PAUL MANSHIP

PAUL MANSHIP

John Manship

Abbeville Press • Publishers • New York

Jacket: Europa and the Bull, *1924*
Detail of plate 95
Pages 1 and 2–3: Fame, *1926*
Pink Georgia marble, 26 x 26 in.
Page 9: Imagination, *1940*
Limestone, 40 x 70 in.
Norton Gallery and School of Art, West Palm Beach, Florida

Editors: Nancy Grubb and Carol A. McKeown
Designer: James Wageman
Picture editor: Lisa Peyton
Production supervisor: Hope Koturo

Library of Congress Cataloging-in-Publication Data

Manship, John.
  Paul Manship / John Manship.
       p.   cm.
    Bibliography: p.
    Includes index.
    ISBN 1-55850-002-1
    1. Manship, Paul, 1885–1966—Criticism and interpretation.
1. Manship, Paul, 1885–1966. II. Title.
NB237.M3M36   1989   *89-81011*
730'.92'4—dc19   *CP7CIP*

CONTENTS

PREFACE

Four years ago I wrote a short biography of my father for the catalog of the exhibition *Paul Manship—Changing Taste in America,* which was organized by the Minnesota Museum of Art. After writing that piece largely from memory, I was inspired to do some research on my father's life, which revealed a number of inaccuracies in what I had written. This book is intended to make amends for those and to complete  what I hope will be seen as an act of filial respect and affection. But, in the belief that truth is sacred, I have not deliberately kept anything secret nor tried to gloss over certain details of his life. With the light heightened by the shadows, the total picture will, I'm sure, be one of a life of remarkable dedication and goodness. One major problem has been deciding what mode to use. Should I write a memoir in the first person, as Jean Renoir did in his book on his father, or should I write an objective life in the third person? I have opted for the latter. It seemed more reasonable, as I do not appear until halfway through the story, nor is my role in the tale of any great importance.

Like many sons, I became closer to my father as we both grew older. By the 1950s we were quite close. We would travel together, visit museums, talk at length about art, my own and his, and the great issues of art in general. I lived in his studio when I was in New York, and he stayed with me in Rome. When he died, I found that I had been named executor of his estate and was responsible for cataloging his work and for disposing of it according to the terms of his will. As time has gone by, I seem to have become increasingly involved in questions concerning his art, and I find myself called upon to authenticate his work or to denounce misattributions and palpable fakes.

1 **JOHN MANSHIP,** *1032
Marble, height: 14½ in.
John and Margaret
Manship*

2 *John Manship*
PAUL MANSHIP, *1005
Oil on canvas, 36 x 20 in.
National Portrait Gallery,
Smithsonian Institution,
Washington, D.C.; Gift
of the artist*

In writing this book I've used whatever material seemed relevant: memoirs by persons who knew my father, letters, and documents. I've studied some of the papers at the Archives of American Art, Smithsonian Institution, but most are in my possession—twelve file cases of them. I've delved deeply into these and, of course, into my own memories. I've been particularly fortunate to have a group of tapes made by my brother-in-law Edwin Murtha, who interviewed my father in the 1960s with the thought of doing a ghostwritten autobiography. But I've had bad luck in interviewing some of the pivotal people in my father's life. His assistant Herbert Lewis Kammerer, for instance, died just as I was preparing to interview him. Next to the architect Eric Gugler and the artist Barry Faulkner, he was probably my father's closest professional colleague. And the sculptor Reuben Nakian, who would certainly have had precious memories of his years working with my father on Washington Mews, died before I had a chance to talk to him. Some of those who did help include: Ferdinand Eiseman, Eric Gugler's partner, who clarified several aspects of their friendship and professional interactions; the sculptor Walker Hancock; my cousins from Minnesota—William Manship, Margaret Manship, and Mary Etta Klatt—who were helpful about the family background in Saint Paul; and my sisters Pauline Natti—whose recent death cut short any hope of further probing her memories—Elizabeth Solomon, and especially Sarah Jane Murtha, who with her husband, Edwin, has been particularly helpful. My wife, Margaret Cassidy, had met my father in Bruno Bearzi's foundry in Florence ten years before she met me, and she has been patient and helpful with suggestions and support. I should also thank the genealogist Walter Arps, who helped in straightening out the Manship background in Maryland; and Claire Stein and Theodora Morgan, of the National Sculpture Society in New York, who let me study the society's files. Susan Rather, in her 1986 doctoral dissertation on Manship, unearthed some material I was unaware of. We are all indebted to her research.

PAUL MANSHIP

1 · A CHILDHOOD IN MINNESOTA

The earliest known reference to the name Manship is in the Domesday Book of 1086. The name—which is Saxon and seems to be native to Yorkshire—derives from the Old English *gemaenscipe*, meaning a "community or fellowship," and denotes land held in common. The first Manship in the New World was Richard, who came from England to the eastern shore of Maryland in 1652 with his wife, Elizabeth; a son, Richard, Jr.; and three daughters. The American Manships are probably descended from

Richard, Jr.[1] One of these was Noah Manship, a Methodist minister and soldier in the War of 1812, who in 1810 married the widow Rebecca Sangston Millington. They had six children, of whom the second—born in 1812— was Charles Henry. While a young man Charles Henry Manship apprenticed to his uncle Samuel Manship, a Balti-more cabinetmaker from whom he learned the skills of a decorative artist: graining, marbling, stenciling, and gilding. In the 1830s Charles migrated to the new state of Mississippi in search of work. He took a coastal boat to New Orleans, a riverboat to Natchez, Mississippi, and finished the journey to Jackson—the new state capital—on foot. The state had embarked on an ambitious building program in Jackson, with the construction of the state capitol and a handsome mansion for the governor. Manship worked on both these structures for the builder David Daley, and in time he married Daley's daughter Adeline. Their eldest son, one of fifteen children, was born in 1843. He, too, was named Charles Henry.

Charles Henry, Sr., became an important figure in Jackson. He was mayor during the Civil War, when the city was besieged by the troops of General Sherman, and after the war he became postmaster. To serve in this federal post,

3 *Charles H. Manship and Adeline Daley Manship, with their sons Charles, Jr. (left), and David, c. 1850*

4 *The Manship family assembled in Jackson, Mississippi, for the golden wedding anniversary of Charles H. Manship and Adeline Daley Manship (at center), 1888. Paul Manship, age two and a half, sits apart on the left.*

he had to receive an official pardon from President Andrew Johnson for his seditious activity in having supported the Confederacy. He operated a decorating business, importing wallpapers and fabrics, and thus became something of a local tastemaker. Before the war he had built his family a handsome Gothic Revival house, profusely decorated with gingerbread, which fortunately survived the burning of Jackson by Sherman's soldiers. It is now on the National Register and, after careful restoration, has been opened to the public as a house museum.

Charles Henry, Jr., was eighteen when the Confederate states seceded from the Union, and he volunteered to fight for the South. Once the war was over, he realized that his prospects at home were none too good, so he went north as far as a Mississippi riverboat would take him. That was to Saint Paul, Minnesota, and there he settled. It's hard to grasp today how new so many things were in the nineteenth century. When Charles Manship arrived in Saint Paul, around 1867, the city was only a dozen years old, and its boomtown atmosphere excited him. On July 22, 1869, he wrote to his family in Jackson: "It would do your heart good to see the rapid strides progress is making in St. Paul. From seven in the morning until six in the evening, the sound of the pick, the hammer, the chisel and the blasting of rock is heard on all sides—never before in its young life has St. Paul known so much building as at the present season. Fine and costly buildings are being erected, which denotes wealth and permanence. If dear old Jackson was only doing a little of this, I would have some hope for her future. The news I have from there is anything but encouraging." If Charles had been hoping to encourage some of his family to venture north, he was to be disappointed, for they all remained in Jackson.

Restlessness seemed to characterize nineteenth-century Americans. They were always moving to improve their lot—or to escape the consequences of their ill fortune. Charles Manship moved from Mississippi to Minnesota; his father-in-law, Kennedy Turner Friend, was born in western Maryland. He had been a general practitioner, but after relocating from Hagerstown, Maryland, to Pittsburgh he opened a bank. He and his large family lived prosperously there for a few years until the depression of 1855, when his bank failed. The Friends then renewed their travels, going by riverboat to Saint Paul.

In 1870 the youngest of the Friends' unmarried daughters, Mary Etta (who had been born in Pittsburgh in 1844), married Charles Manship, who now had a job with the Saint Paul Gas and Light Company. They were to have seven children. The first was William (1871–1942), followed by Charles Henry III (1872–1899), Adeline (1874–1893), Albert (1876–1933), Luther (1879–1931), and Mary

5 *Mary Etta Friend*

6 *Charles H. Manship, Jr.*

Etta (1881–1961). The last was Paul Howard (1885–1966), who later commented on what a good omen it was to be the seventh child of a seventh daughter. He was born on Christmas Eve at the family home at 304 Nelson Avenue. (For a long time he believed that he had been born on Christmas Day; his mother probably practiced this mild deception to avoid giving birthday parties while preparing the Christmas festivities.) When Paul was born, his father was forty-two and his mother, forty-one. Always very conscious of being the child of older parents, he recalled his father as kind but stern and rather distant.[2]

In later years Paul rarely spoke about his siblings, except for Mary, to whom he was very close. Charles Henry III spent most of his short life in an institution; Addie's life was even shorter, for she died of heart failure when she was only nineteen. Paul was only seven at the time, but he remembered her as having been quite beautiful, with a talent for drawing. Albert left for the state of Washington sometime in the 1890s; Mary also moved there after her marriage. Luther remained in Saint Paul after he married, but only William was still living in the family home during the latter part of Paul's youth. Charles Manship remained close to his family in Jackson, and on the occasion of his parents' golden wedding anniversary in 1888, he took his wife and children south to meet the grandparents, aunts, uncles, and cousins.

While the Manships were far from rich, they lived comfortably. They had a pleasant house and yard in the city plus a summer cottage on Bald Eagle Lake, which played an important role in the children's lives. Paul sailed on the lake with his brothers, and they would go fishing and duck hunting. The family kept a cow and chickens, which were largely Paul's responsibility; in the spring he would walk the cow to Bald Eagle and in the fall walk her back to Saint Paul—a distance of about a dozen miles. Paul liked to tell his own children that to get to school he had to trudge great distances through the snow; while there may have been some exaggeration in this, the trip in subzero weather would certainly have been no pleasure, especially since, like most boys, Paul didn't like school very much. What he really liked were the summers at the lake. Some episodes from his childhood: a sudden tornado, when he hurriedly tied up the cow and prayed, "Please, God, remember this little fella." Another time he was out on the lake with a girl when a storm came up and capsized their boat; they managed to make it to an island, where they stayed until help came in the morning.

Paul had many friends, including Tony (Nathaniel) Pousette (later Pousette-Dart), who shared his ambition to succeed as an artist, and Frank van Sloun, who would become a painter. Paul began to draw in emulation of his sister Addie, but it was particularly his brother Luther who served as an example: Luther earned his living as an engraver but his main interest was painting. Paul began to paint too, and he attended Mechanics Arts High School, where in addition to the regular academic subjects he studied mechanical drawing—a skill he would later find useful. Most important, he was introduced to modeling there, a discovery that would determine his future. His parents encouraged him and sent him to study evenings at the one art school in the city, the Saint Paul School of Art (later the Saint Paul Institute of Arts and Sciences).

When Paul was in his junior year in high school, his poor academic record caught up with him. He was failing German, and the principal told the Manships that their son would either have to make up the course or leave school. Paul was not unhappy about this ultimatum—he could already see that his future was in art—but he had to convince his father. After a tense discussion Paul prevailed: his father agreed to let him leave school and try his luck earning his living as an artist. He had already earned some money doing drawings and lettering for advertising cards, a fact that no doubt helped him argue his case. At the age of seventeen, Paul Manship became a free-lance artist, and he never looked back.

During these two years, 1903–5, Manship continued his evening classes at the Institute; during the day he hustled for whatever jobs he could find. His business card, printed to his own design, read: "Paul H. Manship, illustrator and designer, 268½ Robert Street, St. Paul," with a picture in Art Nouveau style of a jester drawing a parrot. He made advertising cards for the streetcars and did some drawings for a firm of engravers at a salary of twenty-five dollars a week. His best job, which earned him between three and four hundred dollars, was illustrating a book by a local doctor on germs and disease. (He used the doctor's microscope to see what he was supposed to draw.) Since he was still living at home, he was able to save most of the money he earned, and these savings would eventually enable him to leave Saint Paul.

At the Institute, Manship was still studying drawing and painting as well as modeling, but his interest was turning increasingly to the latter. It was at this time that he became aware he was color-blind, suffering from a common insensitivity to red and green. He would tell various stories about how this was revealed to him. According to one, he painted a landscape with a field of bright red grass. According to another (recounted in an October 9, 1956, interview for the Columbia University Oral History program), he was painting a still life with a brown jug when Luther asked him why he had painted the jug green. Paul defended himself by invoking artistic license, but in fact he had thought that he was matching the jug's true color. For a painter color blindness is obviously a severe handicap, but for a sculptor it might prove an advantage: the eye, not being distracted by color, could concentrate on form. Indeed, a great sensitivity to form, to contour, and to line was to prove one of Manship's major strengths.

Early in 1905 the nineteen-year-old Manship decided that he had saved up enough money to get a start on his career, and he said good-bye to his family and friends. He would never see his mother again, and during the subsequent sixty years he would return to Minnesota only for short visits. He boarded a train for New York and the great world of art.

2 · THE ART STUDENT

Before deciding on New York, Paul had considered going to Chicago. The second city was much closer to home, and it offered an excellent art school at the Art Institute. But New York was where the major artists lived and worked, so that was where he got off the train. He immediately signed up for classes at the Art Students League, where he studied sculpture with Herman MacNeil—the first of several Beaux-Arts–trained sculptors with whom Manship was to study—and drawing with George  Bridgman, a celebrated anatomist who taught at the League for more than forty years. Mac- Neil's assistant and class monitor was Jo David- son, later the most suc- cessful portrait sculptor of his time. Manship, who became a close friend, always credited Davidson with being the first to show him how to build an armature—one of a young sculptor's most important lessons. Manship tried to make his small savings stretch as far as possible in New York. For instance, he frequented bars that offered a free lunch with a nickel glass of beer. Even so, after a few months he knew he would have to find work. In the spring of 1905 Manship did get a job, which paid two dollars a week, as studio assistant to the sculptor Solon Borglum. Well known for his western themes, particularly depictions of American Indians, Borglum was a westerner, originally from Utah, and had been trained as a sculptor in Paris. He was habitually a loner, but the fact that he had two major public commissions to execute probably accounts for his hiring Manship. Once summer arrived, Bor- glum moved his work from his studio at 30 East Fourteenth Street to a rented house and barn in Mamaroneck, New York. Paul moved in with the Borglums and thus was able to save much of his salary.[3]

7 *Solon Borglum*

8 **MAN WITH WILD HORSES**, *1907*
Detail of plate 12

Borglum had two equestrian monuments to do: one of the Confederate general John B. Gordon, for Atlanta, the other of Captain William Owen O'Neill of the Rough Riders, for Prescott, Arizona. It was an exciting lesson for the young Manship to be involved in the creation of two major sculptures, and it sparked a desire to do his own equestrian sculptures. He later admitted that he had exaggerated his experience and abilities when he had applied for work, but Borglum was a kindly man and a natural teacher. He became a kind of adopted father to Manship, who was always to say that Borglum

9 *Paul Manship with his sculpture* Pulling, *in Solon Borglum's studio, 1906*

was the master who had most influenced him. As studio assistant, Manship kneaded the balls of clay and passed them to Borglum; he swept the studio, mixed plaster, and did a variety of chores for the family. When the two monuments were ready to be cast in plaster, Borglum employed Attilio Contini to do the work. Manship helped mix the plaster and established a friendship with the Continis (Attilio and his son Cesare) that was to last a lifetime.

Manship fervently wanted either to study at the Académie des Beaux-Arts in Paris, as Borglum had done, or to become a disciple of Auguste Rodin. Emma Borglum, who was French, decided that her husband's young assistant should learn French if he wanted to go to Paris, so she had him translate—under her direction—a French book on the anatomy of domestic animals. This was an appropriate choice since Borglum was known as a masterful sculptor of horses; having grown up on a ranch, he knew the animals well. Whenever any animal (including a couple of horses) in the neighborhood died, he and Manship would dissect it to study the attachments of the muscles. While working for Borglum, Manship himself modeled a pair of horses from sketches he had made while observing a team pulling a sand scoop in a pit. He called the piece *Pulling* (plate 9), and it was his first success, featured in the February 1907 issue of the *Western Architect* together with Borglum's *General Gordon.* The *St. Paul Pioneer* ran a photograph of it in 1906 with the caption ''Creditable Sculpture by a St. Paul Youth.'' Manship entered the piece in the National Academy of Design exhibition of 1907, and it was accepted—his first work ever to be shown in a national exhibition.

Manship was modeling animals exclusively at this time. His first commission was of a small bulldog, and he also did a study of the Borglums' dalmatian. A small piece called *Dog Gnawing a Bone* (plate 10), thought to have been lost, has recently reappeared in a private collection in Connecticut. Observing Manship's interest in dogs, Borglum suggested that they dissect one, and Paul enthusiastically agreed. The story of what happened next was one he loved to tell. He procured a dog's body from a local pound, put it in a gunnysack, and headed by streetcar back to the Borglums' place in Mamaroneck. It was a fall evening, and there was no one else on the car but the motorman and the conductor. When he rang the bell to get off, he noticed a big pool of blood under the gunnysack. Fearing that this might be misconstrued (as axe murderers and such were then in the news), he panicked and grabbed the bag, leaping off the car and dashing into the woods to hide. The conductor walked back to see what was going on and spied the blood. He yelled to the motorman, who braked the car and ran back to see what was wrong. The two of them debated what to do but decided

10 **DOG GNAWING A BONE**, *1907*
Plaster
Private collection

not to give chase, and when all was quiet a frightened Manship walked home. The two sculptors performed their dissection, and the knowledge of animal anatomy gained under Borglum's guidance would prove very useful in Manship's later work.

In the fall of 1905 Borglum took his wife and two young children to Paris to visit her family. It may have been during this time that Manship worked for Solon's brother Gutzon, a stay so short that Paul used to joke about it. Paul was at heart a miniaturist and a perfectionist, but Gutzon already suffered from the megalomania and gigantism that were to lead him to Mount Rushmore. He told Paul to go, saying that some sculptors were real men and some were only mice and that he feared Manship would never be anything but a mouse.

The Solon Borglums had been looking for a house in the country, and in the summer of 1906 they found what they wanted. It was an old farm with a hay barn in the village of Silvermine, Connecticut, which straddles the townships of New Canaan, Wilton, and Norwalk. Silvermine later became known as an artists' colony—largely due to Borglum's friends—but in 1906 it was still a farming village, seemingly far removed from the city. By now Manship was like one of the Borglum family, and he helped them with the move. The barn was set up as a studio, and he was given a room there. The Borglums kept a small farm with a vegetable garden, a cow, a horse, pigs, and chickens. Paul helped with chores, as he had at Bald Eagle Lake, milking the cow and gathering eggs.

In the summer of 1907 the Borglums invited a young lady named Isabel McIlwaine to visit. They had first met her in Paris when she was still a girl and Borglum was an art student. The David McIlwaines were from Wheeling, West Virginia, where McIlwaine had a successful business importing bicycle tubing. In the 1890s he had decided to move his whole family to Paris, where they would be relatively near his only son, Frank, who was in boarding school in Switzerland. Isabel, the third of four girls, was placed in a convent school in Fontainebleau, and the family settled in a handsome apartment near the Bois de Boulogne. It was there that Borglum had gone to call, with a letter of introduction from Alfred T. Goshorn, the McIlwaines' cousin and a prominent Cincinnati businessman who had served as director of the Philadelphia Centennial in 1876. Borglum presented his fiancée, Emma Vignal, to the McIlwaines, and they became friends.

Since that period, Isabel's family had fallen on hard times. McIlwaine's partner had taken advantage of his being in France and absconded with their assets. McIlwaine felt compelled to pay off all his creditors, and this left little for his family to live on. Isabel was an attractive and buoyant young woman of twenty-four who had been studying art with William Merritt Chase. She and Paul met at the Borglums' and fell in love, announcing their engagement soon afterward.

On September 26, 1907, near the end of Manship's stay with the Borglums, his mother died and was buried in the Union Cemetery in the town of White Bear Lake; Paul could not get home to attend the funeral. Her understanding and encouragement had been very important to him, and he was deeply saddened by the news. Paul was to say that with her death he had passed a kind of climacteric.

Manship was eager to have the experience of formal art school, and by that fall he had saved enough money from the two dollars a week Borglum had paid him to enroll at the Pennsylvania Academy of the Fine Arts in Philadelphia, one of the oldest and best-known art schools in the country. Borglum had no further need of an assistant, having finished his two great equestrians, so it was time for Manship to move on. In October he began to study with Charles Grafly, then America's leading teacher of sculpture. Grafly was particularly well known for his portrait sculpture, but he had also created several major public monuments. His incisive criticism and his ability to inspire students with high idealism had attracted young sculptors to the Academy from all over the country. Albin Polašek recounted that as monitor of Grafly's classes he was supposed to keep out all but the registered students, and he ejected a sandy-haired young man who turned out to be Paul Manship, newly arrived in Philadelphia. The two were to become good friends and to share the experience of the American Academy in Rome.[4]

Manship formed an especially important friendship at this time with William Hunt Diederich, grandson of the painter William Morris Hunt. A talented artist with a remarkable sense of design, Diederich had a magnetic personality and was quite unencumbered with bourgeois scruples: he said and did whatever he chose. In many ways he and Manship were opposites, although they shared talent and a love of art. Manship was scrupulous and conscientious, hard-working and ambitious, while Diederich was impulsive and amoral, self-destructive to an extent, and somewhat mad. He was very attractive to women and very at-

11 *William Hunt Diederich*

12 **MAN WITH WILD HORSES**, *1907*
Plaster

tracted to them, while Manship was by nature a family man. Hunt was a natural genius with a remarkable sense of design; it is a moot point whether he influenced Manship or Manship him. Their friendship certainly enriched them both.

In his interview for the Columbia University Oral History program Manship said that the main value of his season at the Pennsylvania Academy had been the free availability of models. It was at this time that he had started to model figures, having only modeled animals with Borglum. If his statement seems to denigrate Grafly's instruction, it is because Manship later came to dislike the older artist's rather florid kind of sculpture; but Grafly's professionalism must have had considerable influence on Manship early in his career. Diederich recalled that he and Manship were involved in "a certain fragrant episode that certainly did not endear us to the powers that be."[5] Whatever the reason, they left the Academy in the spring of 1908. Paul wanted to see Isabel, of course, but another major motive for leaving school was the need to earn some money.

Back in New York, Manship found a job as studio assistant to the sculptor Isidore Konti, who had come from Vienna with his friend Karl Bitter in the early 1890s to work on the World's Columbian Exposition in Chicago. Afterward he had established his own studio in New York and had a fair amount of success. During the time he was working in Konti's studio, Manship modeled a decorative relief entitled *Man with Wild Horses* (plate 12). He was to show the piece, which bears Konti's influence, at the National Academy of Design, New York.[6]

In July 1908 Manship embarked on the great lark of his youth. He and Diederich were sketching near a dock on the East River one evening when they got into conversation with some Spanish sailors. Impulsively, Diederich said, "Let's go to Spain!" He arranged it by giving the boatswain's mate of an English ship two bottles of whiskey; in exchange the sailor let them occupy bunks in his cabin. The two artists got off in Gibraltar, but since Manship had only fifteen dollars and Diederich was only comparatively richer with around thirty, they couldn't go far. They tramped around the mountains of Andalusia on foot and slept outdoors or in the most modest of inns. They bathed and washed their clothes in mountain streams. They ate bread and figs (whatever cost least), drank wine, and managed to visit Málaga, Granada, and Ronda. Manship did a lot of drawing during that month (plates 13, 14), in a pictorial style that emphasized chiaroscuro. He drew bulls and cows, goats and pigs, buildings and trees— particularly the ancient, gnarled olive trees of the area. He also drew people going about their daily tasks.

As the friends' funds started to run out, they headed back to Gibraltar. Diederich succeeded in procuring some money, and he lent Manship fifteen dollars to get home. Manship paid about ten dollars to go steerage on one of the

13, *Sketches made in Spain,*
14 *summer 1908*
John and Margaret
Manship

old Cunard liners, while Diederich went on to Paris. By befriending the ship's doctor, Manship was able to improve his accommodations; he stayed in the sick bay for the entire ten-day trip. When he landed in New York, Paul "got running again," as he said. Konti gave him back his job, but Isabel was not so forgiving. She was furious with her fiancé for having so thoughtlessly vanished without a word, and she wasn't at all sure that she wanted any further dealings with such a man. Manship asked Konti to intercede for him, and in time Isabel's heart softened and the engagement continued. But she never quite forgave Hunt, whom she blamed for having led her Paul astray.

Early in 1909 Manship signed up as a student of the painter Robert Henri at the New York School of Art.[7] (It may have been Tony Pousette who persuaded him to study with Henri.) It wasn't for long, as Manship had virtually abandoned any interest in painting, and he never mentioned Henri as one of his teachers. However, he became friends with a number of artists in Henri's circle—notably George Bellows, Eugene Speicher, Rockwell Kent, and Leon Kroll.

There was to be a competition in the summer of 1909 to select a sculptor, a painter, and an architect for a three-year fellowship at the American Academy in Rome. Konti urged Manship to apply. The Academy was modeled on the French Academy and had adopted its method of selecting fellows. The young artists were given a subject, free use of models and materials, and told to execute a work within a fixed period of time in a supervised location. The sculpture subject that year was "Rest after Toil," to be treated in a relief about three feet square and to include a man, woman, and child; the judge was the sculptor Daniel Chester French. Work was done in July in the study rooms of the National Academy of Design, where it must have been painfully hot. Ten contestants were narrowed to two, and in the end Manship was declared the winner. One can imagine how delighted he must have been, and Isabel, too, even though she knew this meant their marriage would have to be postponed. The excitement spread to Saint Paul, where the *Pioneer* published a glowing story about the honor accorded its native son. It also reported that he would return home before sailing to Europe.

Back in Saint Paul, Manship experienced again many of the pleasures of his adolescence. He wrote to Konti that he was having the time of his life hunting, fishing, sailing, and motoring with his friends and with his brothers Will and Luther.[8] While Manship was home, Governor John Albert Johnson died suddenly, on September 21. His admirers wanted to have a death mask made and, knowing that Manship had just won a prestigious fellowship, they asked him to do it. Manship accepted with, as he later said, the confidence of ignorance. Luckily, one of his cousins was a dentist used to handling plaster and making molds, so he helped with the mechanics. The two young men worked at night in the great rotunda of Cass Gilbert's state capitol, where the governor's body was lying in state. Manship said later that it was a very eerie experience, but despite their fears, they got the job done.

Paul found his father far from well. Charles Manship had long suffered from asthma (a family affliction that would plague all of his sons), and now it had affected his heart, at the same time that the death of his wife had undermined his will to live. Paul sensed that he would never see his father again. Manship said good-bye to his family and friends in Saint Paul, and it was to be almost sixteen years before he saw any of them again. Once back in New York, he wrote to Daniel Chester French and asked if he might visit him. French was at his country estate in Stockbridge, Massachusetts, but he suggested that Manship go there and spend a night with his family—an invitation the young artist eagerly accepted. Mrs. French described the visit in her memoirs:

> [He] seemed to find so much to interest him in the studio and in the country, which was of course very different from that of his home in the West, that we asked him to spend a few days. Mr. French and in fact all of us were busy, and he claimed that he was quite equal to taking care of himself. He was. I felt that he saw every inch of everything that was in the studio, and every tree and shrub and growing thing on the place. I think of him standing in the middle of the lawn, gazing at the view and clouds, at the air itself, breathing it in. It seemed to me, during those days, that, whenever I looked out of the window, I saw this slim, boyish figure standing somewhere, anywhere, breathing in the beauty which he found everywhere. . . .[9]

The time came for Paul's departure for Rome. He said good-bye to his New York friends, to Konti, to Isabel, and he left for the three years in Europe that were to make such a difference to his life and his work.

3 · THE AMERICAN ACADEMY IN ROME

15 **LYRIC MUSE**, *1012*
Detail of plate 20

The American Academy in Rome was the brainchild of Charles Follen McKim. It is said that while he was working on the plans for the Chicago World's Columbian Exposition of 1893 he became aware of a need for architects, painters, and sculptors who had been trained to work together, and he resolved to found a school where such collaborative training would be offered. The Academy was to be a postgraduate institution, where the elite of American art schools would be free to follow their own artistic goals, with the only requirement being that they do collaborative projects with the Fellows in other disciplines. Each year one architect, one painter, and one sculptor were to be selected for three-year fellowships, so that there would be nine men in residence in the school at any given time. There were to be no women students, and the men were all to be unmarried. Where but Rome could it be? Not only was it the site of the Colosseum and the Ara Pacis, the Villa Madama and the Sistine Chapel, but it had been the home of a comparable school, the French Academy, for three hundred years. McKim got the backing of some of the nation's richest men, including J. P. Morgan and John D. Rockefeller; he established a prestigious board of architects, painters, and sculptors; and in 1897 the Academy was opened.

Paul set sail from New York in September 1909 on the *Lusitania,* bound for England. He stayed a few days in London and in Holland, visiting museums and monuments before traveling on to Paris. In this he was true to form, as all his life he was to be an intrepid museum goer. In Paris he saw a number of Rodin's sculptures, which did not impress him. Rodin's *Victor Hugo* had "stiff fingers," he wrote to Konti, and looked like an imitation of Gutzon Borglum. But he very much liked Constantin Meunier's work.

Paul later wrote that he was unhappy during his first year in Rome. He was homesick, he missed Isabel, and he was having trouble with Italian (though he later learned to speak it very adequately). He was also confused about his own art

and wanted to start anew. His attention was drawn back to Minnesota, in pursuit of a will o' the wisp. The late Governor Johnson, whose death mask he had executed, was to be honored with a sculptural monument, and Manship badly wanted this commission. Although he was a native Minnesotan and had done the death mask, he was young and inexperienced and had few other qualifications. He tried pulling some strings, frustrated at being in Rome. He wrote to Konti, begging him to put in a good word to the committee members, whom he also besieged with letters. He even went so far as to ask Konti whether he should resign his fellowship to go home to get this job.[10] Konti must have advised against such a move, because Manship stayed on in Rome. He did not get the commission, but the loss was ultimately his gain. If he had won the commission, he would have returned to the United States without the experience of Rome and Greece. And without that crucial experience, he would most likely have fallen back on the Beaux-Arts sculptural style of his teachers MacNeil, Borglum, and Grafly. In this affair Paul learned something about the politics and anguish of seeking commissions. The episode reveals the young sculptor's driving ambition: he wanted success, he wanted his place in the world of art, and he would work hard for it.

During Manship's first year in Rome he began a friendship with the mural painter Barry Faulkner that was to last all his life. Faulkner had been at the Academy for two years, although he'd spent much of that time in Florence, working in the studio of his friend and mentor, the painter George de Forest Brush. In his memoirs Faulkner records his first meeting with Manship: "Among the new Fellows at the Academy was Paul Manship, and that summer and fall [1910] we formed a friendship that lasted for more than fifty years. When we first met, Paul, then about twenty-four, was slim, short, and sturdy, and his head was covered with a fuzz of hair on its way to baldness. He was a lyric sculptor whose humor enlivened everything he touched. He possessed an exceptional power of concentration and an ardor for all things connected with sculpture."[11] Faulkner also described a kind of "artistic indigestion" that perhaps best explains Paul's uneasiness during this time: "Rome is an over-rich layer-cake of civilizations and periods in art which if eaten greedily, results in indigestion. After a series of stomach-aches, the shock lessens; [the student's] mind becomes less agitated, and he begins to feel at home with the repose of the Classic and fire of the Baroque."[12]

It's hard to exaggerate the mental turbulence caused by Manship's sudden immersion in great art. What he saw of ancient art—both classical and archaic

Greek, medieval, and Renaissance—was instrumental in the development of his own style. There was a good deal of sculpture being done in Italy at this time, as Rome was being filled with monuments to the Risorgimento, but although he met some contemporary Italian sculptors (he would later mention Arturo Dazzi and Giulio Monteverdi, among others), Manship was in no way influenced by what they were doing. The distant past was his revelation.

At the beginning of his stay Manship modeled a small piece called *End of Day* (plate 16), which portrays a tired farmer leaning against a horse. The piece is in

16 **END OF DAY**, *1907*
Bronze, 8¾ x 10 in.

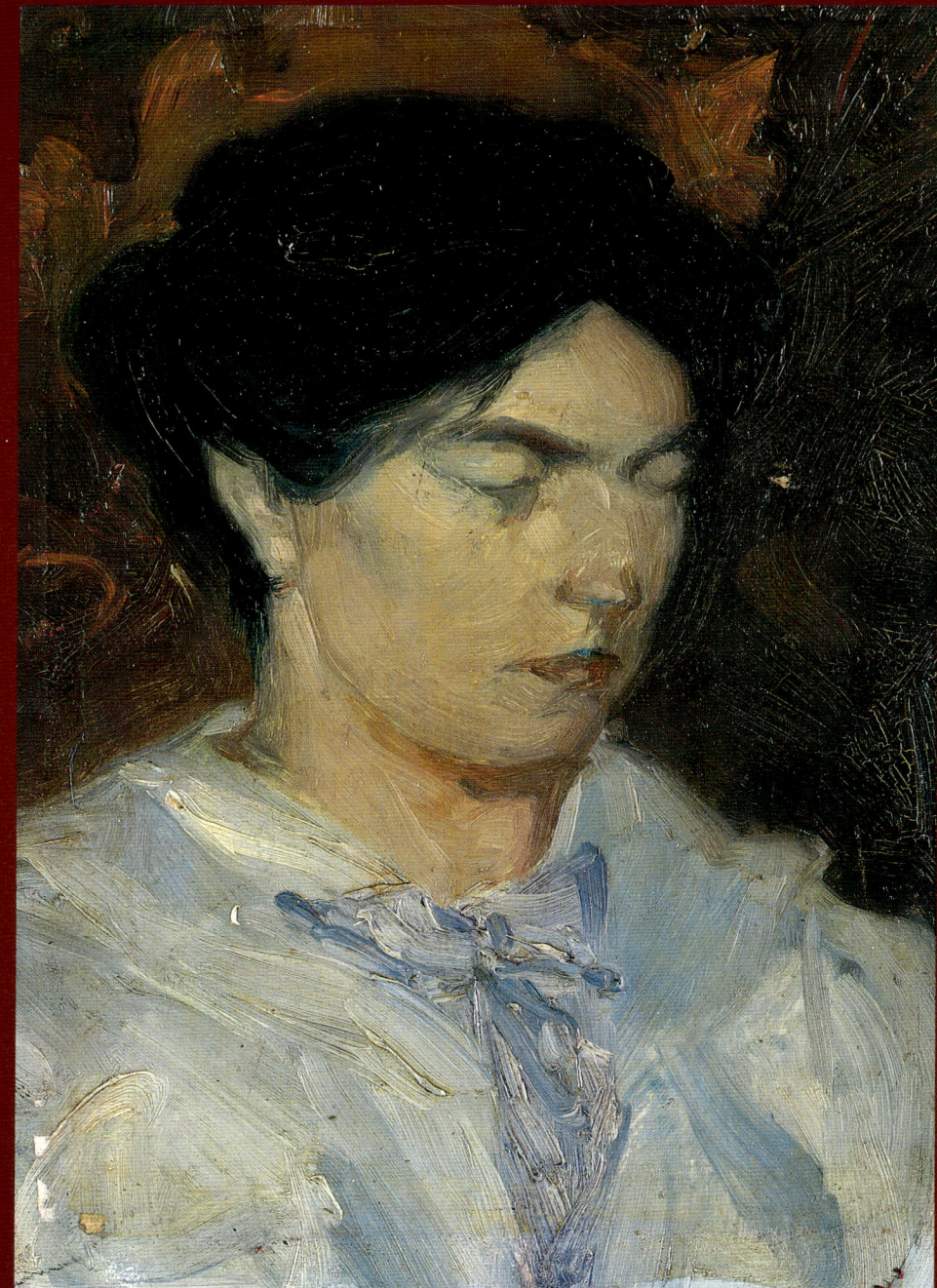

17 **SELF-PORTRAIT** *c. 1910*
Oil on canvas,
10½ x 9½ in.
John and Margaret
Manship

18 **ISABEL McILWAINE**
c. 1910
Oil on canvas,
7½ x 5½ in.
John and Margaret
Manship

the Beaux-Arts style and much influenced by Solon Borglum. During this period Manship also did a number of small paintings: landscapes around Rome and the campagna, a portrait of Isabel (plate 18), and a pair of self-portraits (plate 17; the other of these shows the artist as the Archangel Gabriel in the Annunciation, a spoof of Renaissance painting). Within a year of his arrival in Rome, Manship's work was profoundly marked by the influence of classical art, particularly the Pompeian bronzes in Naples. Photographs taken in his studio in November 1910 and in 1911 (plates 19, 20) show an early stage of the *Centaur and Dryad,* without the strong rhythms of the finished piece (plate 38).

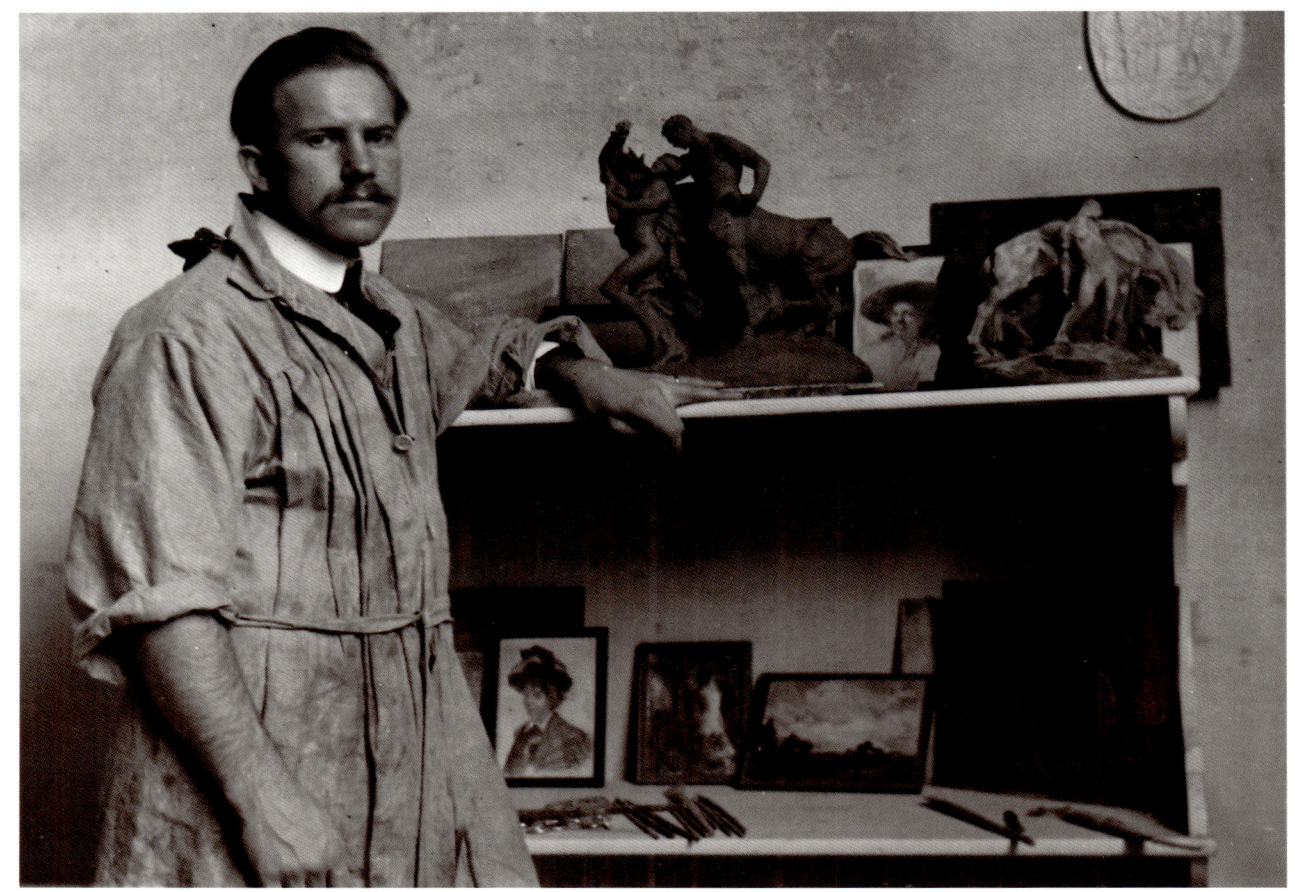

The story of the *Duck Girl* (plate 23) is one that Manship loved to tell. In July 1910 he went to a fair in Rome and played an old Italian game that involved casting a ring over the head of a swimming duck. Paul succeeded with his third throw and claimed the duck as his prize. After the crowds had thinned he carried the duck back to the Academy on the streetcar, concealed under his coat, and tied it to the foot of his bed for the night. The following day, after it had awakened the whole Academy with its quacks, Paul started out for his studio with his prize. But in the garden the duck immediately escaped into the fountain, where the director's wife kept goldfish. It caused all kinds of havoc, with Paul and the other Fellows chasing the poor duck until it was finally caught. When the director asked the young sculptor for an explanation, Paul said that he planned to use the duck as a model for a piece of sculpture, and this was considered an adequate excuse. He had his favorite model, a girl named Marietta, pose holding the duck. The result was a charming and very Pompeian statue, which now stands in Rittenhouse Square in Philadelphia.[13]

As he got used to life in Rome, Manship found it very pleasant indeed. There were certain obligatory duties—the collaborative studies that were the raison d'être of the Academy, which Manship performed with the Fellows of his year,

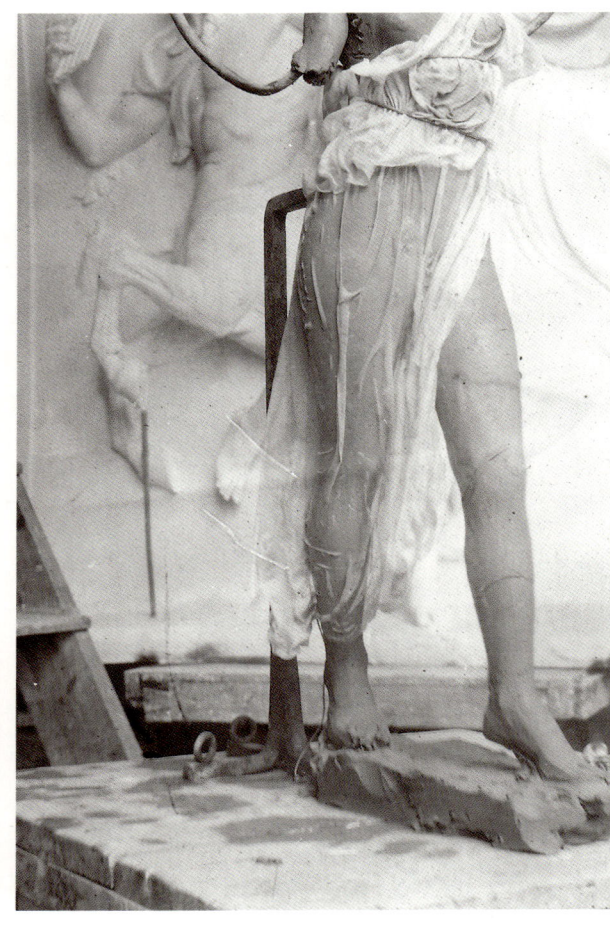

21 *Paul Manship with plaster version of* Duck Girl, *1011*

22 *An early stage of* Duck Girl, *showing wet drapery arranged on the clay figure, 1910. Partially visible behind it is the* Wood Nymph's Dance.

23 **DUCK GIRL**, *1011*
Bronze, height: 50 in.; diameter of base: 34 in. Rittenhouse Square, Philadelphia Given to the city of Philadelphia by the Fairmount Park Art Association

the architect Edgar Williams (brother of the poet William Carlos Williams) and the painter Frank Fairbanks—but otherwise he was free to pursue his own studies. The director of the Academy was Frederic Crowninshield, a distinguished painter from an old and socially prominent Salem family. The other Fellows included the sculptors Sherry Fry of the class of 1908, Albin Polašek of 1910, and Harry Thresher of 1911, and the mural painters F. Tolles Chamberlin and Ezra Winter. The Fellows had social contacts with the resident American artists—such as old Elihu Vedder and the sculptor Moses Ezekiel, whom Manship got to know, as well as the prominent sculptor Frederick William Mac-Monnies, who that year had a studio at the Villa Strohl Fern—as well as with the visiting Americans, notably the Academy trustees. They also got to know the students at some of the other foreign academies; one, the French sculptor Louis Lejeune, was to remain a lifelong friend of Manship's. And, of course, the Fellows enjoyed their own company, dining together in neighborhood restaurants. It was during these years that Paul developed his love of Frascati wine and Roman cuisine. The social life seemed especially brilliant to a somewhat naive boy from Minnesota. In a letter to his brother Will, Paul reported he had gone "to a ball last evening which was the swellest affair that I have ever attended. There were eight princesses, five duchesses, numerous baronesses and marquises at the affair: there was certainly some class at that dance! I danced until four A.M.—one of those balls that commence at eleven—you know," knowing that Will's experience of balls that began at 11 P.M. was slight. Another dramatic moment that he described to Will was an earthquake: "Yesterday while I was in my studio at work I felt the studio quake and on the moment thought it was only the wind—but when I looked around and saw the big mirrors which I had setting on a chair rock back and forth . . . I realized that it was an earthquake and . . . if anything was going to fall I chose to be under the big blue vault and so I ran out into the garden—there I met one of the painters rushing out of his studio followed by a nude young lady—a model who was scared to death."

A particularly happy time came in the summer of 1910, when Isabel McIlwaine sailed to Europe. Isabel had a job reading to her good friend Charis François, a wealthy girl who was losing her eyesight. Isabel, who couldn't possibly have afforded to go to Europe on her own, suggested that they travel together and that she serve as Charis's guide in exchange for her fare. Isabel was, of course, determined not to let three years go by before she saw Paul again. The women went first to Germany, where they saw the passion play at Oberammergau. They then traveled south to Italy, where Paul met them, accompanied by Frank

Fairbanks. Isidore Konti, who was vacationing in Europe, joined them in Venice for a happy reunion. During this summer Charis was facing total blindness, and Frank was recovering from tuberculosis of the hip. He was very lame and habitually used a cane. Perhaps drawn together by their disabilities, Charis and Frank fell in love. Their romance assured Isabel of a return to Italy in 1911. This time the four of them traveled to Verona and Florence, and they saw the running of the Palio in Siena before Isabel had to return to her job teaching. In writing to

24 **WOOD NYMPH'S DANCE**, *1000*
Plaster, life size
Destroyed by the artist

Will, Paul spoke of his eager desire to get married. As soon as his fellowship was over, he would "take the plunge."

One of the few sad notes of this period was Charles Manship's death in Saint Paul on February 2, 1911, two weeks before his sixty-eighth birthday. Supportive of Paul's ambitions and proud of his winning the fellowship, he had helped by sending his son money. Manship's brothers Will and Luther were now the only family left in Saint Paul, and it was Will's duty to settle his father's estate. He wrote to Paul, offering him the cottage at Bald Eagle Lake, but Paul refused it. He said he didn't expect to return to Minnesota and told Will that he should have the cottage himself.

About this time Manship sent Daniel Chester French some photographs of his latest work. In a letter of July 10, 1911, French expressed enthusiastic admiration: "The relief (the *Wood Nymph's Dance* [plate 24]) is beautiful,—beautiful in light and shade and feeling." French strongly advised him to take advantage of his stay in Rome to study ornament. He said that he had always regretted not being more knowledgeable about moldings and the like and had found that a knowledge of ornament was necessary for the architectural sculpture he was so often commissioned to do. Manship certainly heeded his advice: ornament and lettering were to be among his specialties.

In January 1911 Frederic Crowninshield had resigned the directorship of the Academy. He was unhappy with the trustees' decision to merge the Academy in Rome with the American School of Archaeology and to build a permanent home for the combined school on the Janiculum. His replacement was the architect

Gorham Stevens, a member of the firm McKim, Mead, and White. The Fellows presented Mr. and Mrs. Crowninshield with a plaque that Manship had modeled in their honor. It portrayed a winged figure holding in one hand a putto blowing a trumpet and in the other two doves. This was Manship's first effort in the medallic form, a form he was to pursue with great success throughout his life.

In the spring of 1912 Manship went to Greece, where he received the ultimate revelation of these years, the discovery of the beauty, the sinuous and rhythmic grace of early Greek sculpture. This was the inspiration he needed to find his own way. By 1912 the later periods of classical art had, to a large extent, been drained of their inspirational juices. High classical art had inspired the Neoclassical sculptors who, in the wake of Antonio Canova, had dominated their art for more than a century. Franklin Simmons and Moses Ezekiel were, in 1912, the last practitioners of a style graced by Horatio Greenough, Thomas Crawford, Harriet Hosmer, and Hiram Powers more than a half-century before. The Beaux-Arts style, in which Manship had been trained, owed a good deal to the Hellenistic example in its naturalism and in its florid theatricality. But Manship wanted to do something different, and his exposure to archaic Greek sculpture provided the necessary catalyst.

Other sculptors of his generation were discovering archaic or "primitive" art. Eric Gill in England and Ivan Meštrović in Croatia were looking at medieval religious art; Carl Milles in Sweden and Emile-Antoine Bourdelle and Elie Nadelman in France were studying archaic Greek art. The more radical modernists, such as Jacob Epstein, Jacques Lipchitz, and José De Creeft, were looking to the art of Africa or the Pacific Islands for their inspiration. These were developments on the international art scene; Manship was the first American to

25 A corner in Paul Manship's Rome studio, 1912. The plaster models include End of Day *and* Lyric Muse *(top shelf);* Satyr and Sleeping Nymph, Young Minerva, *and* Playfulness *(middle shelf); and* Centaur and Dryad *(bottom shelf). Two of the paintings are self-portraits, including the one as the Archangel Gabriel (above the top shelf). The plaster bust at top left is after a work by Francesco Laurana, whose work the young sculptor admired.*

break away from the Beaux-Arts style. Among these innovative European sculptors, he was probably familiar with only the work of Meštrovič, who exhibited in Rome in 1911.

On May 15, 1912, the Academy hosted a symposium on two subjects of interest to its Fellows: "The Decorative Value of Greek Sculpture," a slide lecture by Manship, and "Velásquez and Impressionism" by Frank Fairbanks. Having just returned from Greece, Paul was filled with the excitement of his discoveries in sculpture and style. In his talk he insisted on the abstract qualities of Greek sculpture. Speaking of the Ludovisi Throne, for instance, he said that "the human figure was considered as a moment, a combination of lines and masses going to decorate the required surface with great directness and simplicity." While he expressed his admiration for the Hermes of Praxiteles, he said that it seemed sweet and sentimental compared to the earlier marbles in Olympia from the Temple of Zeus. But he saved his greatest enthusiasm for the Charioteer of Delphi, one of the few original Greek bronzes then known. The hair, he said, "is executed in most minute detail. The bronze worker was an engraver who guided his tool with the precision of a goldsmith and with a taste for the appropriate in decoration which makes it a jewel of sculpture. Each eyelash is a separate hair of bronze, the eyes are executed in color and are most natural and beautiful; the fillet around his head was decorated with a meander inlaid in silver. All this perfection and delicacy of detail is but secondary to the simplicity and spontaneity—the aristocratic dignity of the type!" After speaking on how the design of a statue relates to that of a building, Manship praised the archaic Greek sculptor: "He considered the relation of each fold to its neighbor, of each mass of drapery to the others—of every feature of the statue with every other in its harmony of shape and size." This is the program that Manship set for himself. He was to become the most artful of sculptors.

As his stay in Rome was nearing its end, Manship created a group of small sculptures that were to establish his reputation when he took them home: *Playfulness* (plate 28), *Lyric Muse* (plate 26), *Little Brother* (plate 27), *Satyr and Sleeping Nymph* (plate 36), and *Centaur and Dryad* (plate 37), now entirely reworked. These pieces display the archaizing treatment of hair and drapery, the jewellike finish, and the rhythmic lyricism of design that he admired in early Greek sculpture and that were to characterize his mature style. He had the *Duck Girl* cast at a foundry in Stuttgart, Germany, using the Galvano process. Thus he was able to take back to New York not only that large bronze but also several other small ones. He took several plasters as well, including the *Wood Nymph's*

26 **LYRIC MUSE**, *1012*
Bronze, height: 11¾ in.;
base: 7 x 5½ in.

27 **LITTLE BROTHER**, *1012*
Bronze, height: 12⅝ in.;
base: 4¹¹⁄₁₆ x 7⅜ in.
Cincinnati Art Museum;
Wilson Fund

Bronze, 12⅝ x 12 x 6⅝
in.; base: 0 x 6¼ in.
The Saint Louis Art
Museum; Museum
Purchase

Above
29 Sketch of Greek sculpture,
Delphi, May 3, 1912

Right
30 Paul Manship working on
Mask of Silenus, 1911

Far right
31 **MASK OF SILENUS**,
1012
Plaster, heroic size
Destroyed by the artist

Dance and a large group called *Mask of Silenus* (plate 31), portraying a nude male holding a child frightened by his mask. Neither of these large plasters was ever cast in bronze, and both were eventually destroyed.

Paul's fellowship was over in the fall of 1912. His three years in Italy had been absolutely crucial to his career but he was eager to return to the States. Although he was often to live and travel abroad, he never had a desire for permanent expatriation, unlike his friend Frank Fairbanks, who had now married Charis and settled in Europe. Manship's brother Will had finally married, after many letters from Paul chiding him for remaining a bachelor so long. And Paul and Isabel would be married soon.

4 · TRIUMPH

When Paul returned to New York in the fall of 1912, there was much for him to do. His years in Rome had permitted him the leisure to study, to work, and to mature in a rich cultural environment, and one where all his economic needs had been met. It was during this time that he evolved into an artist, producing work that was distinctly his own. But now that he was back in New York, earning a living had become a high priority. He had to find himself a studio and a place to live, and he had to make arrangements for his wedding. He took a studio at 27 Lexington Avenue, at the corner of Twenty-third Street, in a building where Augustus Saint-Gaudens had once had his studio.

C. Grant La Farge, son of the painter John La Farge and secretary of the American Academy in Rome, was aware of Manship's work and offered him a commission as soon as the young sculptor returned to New York. An architect of considerable distinction who specialized in designing churches, La Farge was working on the Roman Catholic Church of the Blessed Sacrament in Providence, Rhode Island, for which he had Manship produce a statue of Saint Joseph (plate 33). This was the only religious sculpture of consequence in Manship's long career. It is a standing figure, just under life-size, holding a lily (as mandated by tradition). In conceiving this piece, Paul was flooded by memories of the exquisite sculptures of the Florentine Renaissance, particularly the work of Benedetto da Maiano, a particular favorite of his. Manship's *Saint Joseph* fits into the style art historians have named the American Renaissance. At this time McKim, Mead, and White were still building Florentine-style palaces in New York, and the mural painters Albert Herter and H. Siddons Mowbray, as well as Ezra Winter and Barry Faulkner in their earliest work, were reinterpreting the great painted rooms of fifteenth-century Italy. Yet even in this work, as in all the eclectic creations of Manship's early career, one is aware of a contemporary intelligence and personality.

32 **CENTAUR AND DRYAD**, *1012*
Detail of plate 38

Daniel Chester French was another trustee of the Academy who was particularly interested in Manship's work. French had been engaged by the Danville, Illinois, chapter of the Daughters of the American Revolution to do a monument to the Revolutionary soldiers buried in Vermilion County. The commission was not a particularly important one, and French was at the height of his career, so he designed the memorial in collaboration with his friend the architect Henry Bacon and asked Manship to model the statue. Manship's depiction of a young soldier (plate 34) was cast in bronze and placed atop a shaft surrounded by a semicircular fountain with stone benches on either side.

These two unsought but welcome commissions guaranteed a sufficient income for Paul and Isabel to set a date for their wedding. The simple ceremony was performed on January 1, 1913, in the chantry of Grace Episcopal Church at Tenth Street and Broadway, where Isabel was a member. Isidore Konti was best man and Frances Howard, a friend of Isabel's from Baltimore, was maid of honor. Paul, in his excitement, failed to acquire a top hat and had to borrow one

33 **SAINT JOSEPH**, *1013*
Plaster, nearly life size

34 **SOLDIER OF THE REVOLUTIONARY WAR**, *1013*
Plaster, nearly life size

at the last minute from Barry Faulkner. Isabel, who always remained extremely fond of Barry, liked to joke that she was married to his hat. It was a small wedding, with only a few friends in attendance, and there was no question of a honeymoon. Paul was busy with his two commissions and with completing the work he had brought back from Rome for his forthcoming exhibition. It was also impossible to leave Isabel's father, who was bedridden from a stroke and came to live with them in their new apartment at 1142 Madison Avenue.[14]

In February 1913 the American Academy in Rome reserved a gallery at the Architectural League in New York to exhibit the work of the three Fellows who had returned the preceding fall. Manship showed ten pieces done in Rome, eight of which were in bronze: the *Duck Girl* (plate 23), *Centaur and Dryad* (plate 38), *Playfulness* (plate 28), *Little Brother* (plate 27), *Lyric Muse* (plate 26), *Young Minerva* (plate 35; later called *Marietta,* after the model who had posed for it), *Satyr and Sleeping Nymph* (plate 36), and the Crowninshield medallion. The other two were large works in plaster: *Mask of Silenus* (plate 31) and the *Wood*

Left

36 **SATYR AND SLEEPING NYMPH**, 1012
Bronze, height: 10 in.;
base: 17½ x 8 in.

Below

37 **CENTAUR AND DRYAD**, 1013
Plaster, 20 x 21½ in.

Opposite

38 **CENTAUR AND DRYAD**, 1013
Bronze, 20 x 21½ in.
The Metropolitan
Museum of Art, New
York; Amelia B. Lazarus
Fund, 1914

Nymph's Dance (plate 24). The response to the exhibition was remarkable. Manship was praised by the influential Charles H. Caffin in the *New York Evening Journal* on February 13, 1913; and in the February 1913 issue of the *Nation* there was a long article entitled "A New Sculptor" by Kenyon Cox, which more than anything else helped launch Manship. The continuing backing of Cox, a leading Academician, was very valuable to the young sculptor. Also in April, a three-page piece in *Century* reproduced the Crowninshield medallion, *Playfulness,* and the *Duck Girl.* Curiously, in none of this press coverage were the names of the coexhibitors even mentioned.

During the summer of 1913 the Manships traveled to Oakland, Maryland, to visit Isabel's friend Frances Howard, but otherwise they stayed in New York: Paul was increasingly busy, and Isabel was pregnant. On December 22 Pauline Frances was born and named for her father and for Frances Howard. Paul was ecstatic about her arrival and promptly made a medal for Isabel (plate 39), who later was to say that she was one of the few women ever awarded a medal for giving birth.

It had been a banner year for Manship: not only had he been married at its beginning and become a father at its end, but his successful first exhibition in February had been followed by two more in November.[15] One was a private showing in his studio on Lexington Avenue and the other was a group show of American sculptors at the Gorham Gallery. These later shows included a few new pieces: *Yawning* (also called *Spring Awakening),* a figurine of a nude girl stretching and yawning as she awakens; a small portrait statuette of his sister-in-law Jeannette McIlwaine (his first contemporary subject; plate 41); and a bronze vase with an Oriental dancer in low relief (plate 42). The vase was the first of his works to show a new influence, that of Oriental art.

On December 5 Manship signed a contract with the philanthropist Herbert L. Pratt, who had seen and liked the *Duck Girl*, to produce two life-size sculptures for niches in the garden wall of Pratt's home in Glen Cove, Long Island. One of these was a cast of the *Duck Girl*; the other was to be a male figure. The fee for both was seven thousand dollars—a large sum in 1913. The male figure, which was done within a year, was the first in a series of hunters by Manship. Called *Spirit of the Chase* (plate 43; also known as *The God of Hunting*), it depicts a young man, nude to the waist, with a boar skin covering his lower body.

On December 13 Kenyon Cox informed Manship that the jury of the National Academy had voted unanimously to award the Helen Foster Barnett Prize— then the only prize for sculpture offered by the Academy—for his *Centaur and Dryad*. The New York press reported the event, and other newspapers throughout the country picked up the story, including the *St. Paul Pioneer*, whose headline read, "St. Paul Man among the World's Great Sculptors."

40 *Paul Manship's studio at 27 Lexington Avenue, arranged for his exhibition, November 0–8, 1013*

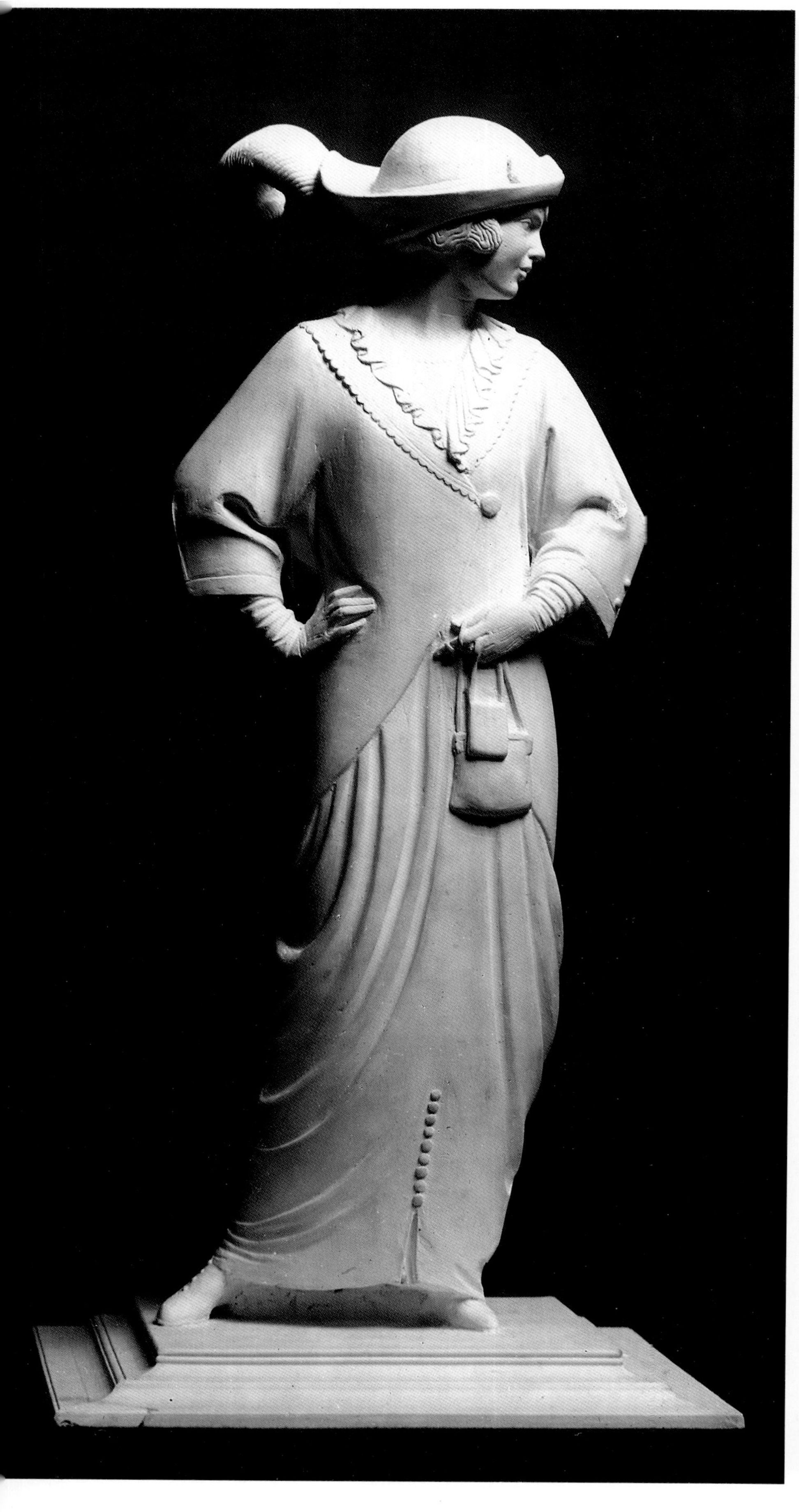

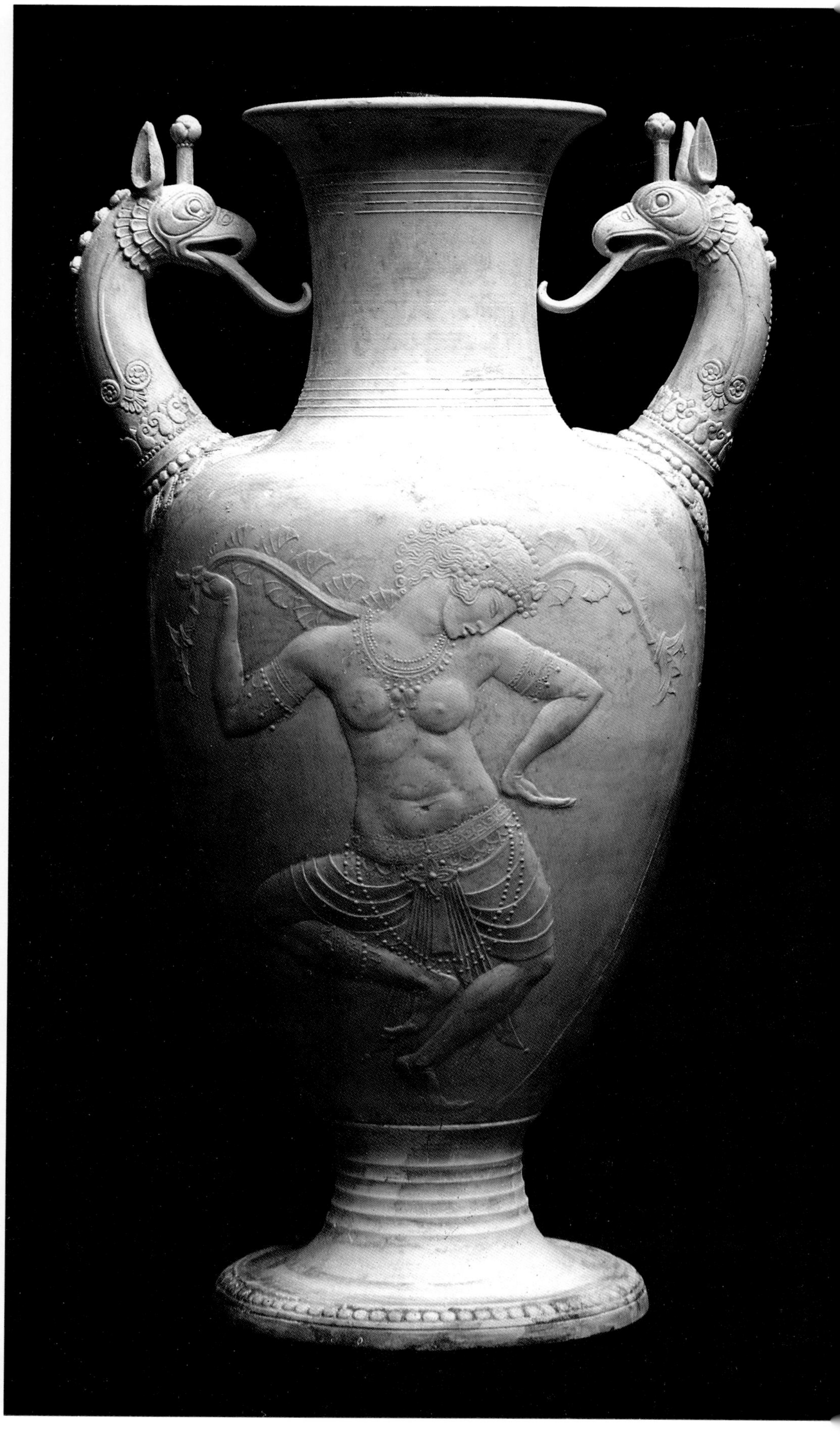

On Christmas Day 1913 Paul had much to be grateful for: a loving wife, a healthy baby, adequate finances, and a remarkable start to a successful career. He had just turned twenty-eight.

Everything seemed to serve Manship's rising celebrity. *Metropolitan Magazine* ran a four-page spread in February 1914 on his sculpture, with reproductions of the *Satyr and Sleeping Nymph, Centaur and Dryad,* the *Wood Nymph's Dance,* and *Playfulness.* This in itself was excellent publicity for the young sculptor, but the effect was much intensified when the postmaster of New York City ruled that the magazine could not be sent through the mail on grounds of obscenity. "There is no doubt in my mind the pictures are indecent," Postmaster Edward Morgan is reported to have said. "The one of the *Centaur and Dryad* is bestial. It depicts the leering passions of a monster. The one of the *Wood Nymph's Dance* is a Centaur pursuing a girl and is something I would not permit in my family circle. The *Metropolitan Magazine* may call me the Puritan Postmaster, but by the time I get through with them they may not be so anxious to publish pictures of this sort."[16]

The magazine's publisher reacted immediately, of course, and quickly got the postal authorities in Washington to rescind the postmaster's order. But the fat was already in the fire, with civil libertarians and art lovers lined up against the defenders of public morals. In the meantime *Metropolitan Magazine* sold more copies than it ever had, and the name Paul Manship became well known in circles only marginally interested in contemporary sculpture. The *San Diego Union* (February 1, 1914) carried a long story attacking the zealous postmaster; the *New York Tribune* (January 21, 1914) noted that one of the offensive sculptures—*Centaur and Dryad*—had been bought by John D. Rockefeller, who was not known for collecting pornography.[17] The *Baltimore American* (March 4, 1914) reported that *Metropolitan Magazine* was bringing suit for $100,000 against Postmaster Morgan, but his actions had already been worth much more than that to them.

Manship's defenders spoke of the chastity of these works, but that may be something of an exaggeration. The pieces are undeniably sexy: the centaur is pawing the coquettish dryad, who is making a very halfhearted effort to escape; the satyr is tickling the ear of the sleeping nymph. After all, these are the works of a young bachelor whose engagement to a girl he wholeheartedly loved had been extended by more than three years. No wonder he had sex on his mind. That his nature was nonetheless essentially domestic is evidenced by the number

44 **PAULINE FRANCES—
THREE WEEKS OLD**,

*1914
Marble and polychromed
bronze, height: 27 in.
The Metropolitan
Museum of Art, New
York; Gift of Mrs.
Edward F. Dwight, 1016*

of his pieces in which children figure. The children in *Playfulness* and *Little Brother* are miniature adults, with long, muscular bodies and small heads. But Paul now had a child of his own and he lost no time in portraying his baby daughter. *Pauline Frances—Three Weeks Old* (plate 44) is a masterpiece. The work captures with great sensitivity the baby's fragility and her dawning awareness of the world. The marble sculpture, in its ornate frame, is the final expression of Manship's love of Renaissance art and a masterful evocation of the

quattrocento. The portrait was exhibited at the National Academy and with other pieces in Philadelphia, and then it was purchased in 1916 by Mrs. E. H. Dwight for the Metropolitan Museum of Art in New York. The museum had already acquired *Centaur and Dryad* at the urgent insistence of Daniel Chester French, who served as a special advisor to the Department of American Art and was

primarily responsible for developing the museum's exceptional collection of American sculpture.

In February 1914 Manship exhibited thirteen of his sculptures at his old school, the Pennsylvania Academy of the Fine Arts, and the *Duck Girl* was awarded the George D. Widener Memorial Gold Medal for sculpture. The family went down to Philadelphia on February 8 for the award with—as Isabel put it—the three B's: Barry, Bozzy (William Welles Bosworth), and Baby. Manship's new pieces—the portrait of baby Pauline, the statuette of Jeannette McIlwaine, and the *Indian* and *Pronghorn Antelope* (plate 45)—attracted particular attention. The last-mentioned pair had been done in bronze for the couple's own mantelpiece, and it represents the first in a long series of American Indian figures in Manship's oeuvre. The following week the Civic Forum of New York awarded to George Washington Goethals, the engineer of the Panama Canal, its first gold medal—a medal designed by Manship. One side showed Columbia holding a winged Victory, and the other, an eagle.

Bozzy—the architect William Welles Bosworth—had commissioned Manship in January to make six terra-cotta flower boxes (plate 46) for John D. Rockefeller's residence on West Fifty-fourth Street in Manhattan. Having recently completed the main buildings of the new campus at his alma mater, the Massachusetts Institute of Technology, in Cambridge, Bosworth was now designing the headquarters for the American Telephone and Telegraph Company at Broadway and Fulton Street in New York. The building was a masterpiece of classical design, a skyscraper with the stylistic elements of a Greek temple, and no expense was to be spared in its ornamentation. Bosworth asked Manship to model a number of pieces for this building, including a drinking fountain, a door pull (plate 47), a frieze in low relief of children with garlands (which was later extended by Gaston Lachaise), a pair of large floor plaques in bronze (plate 48), and four intricately detailed reliefs symbolizing the four elements (plates 50–53).

Although these reliefs were not installed in the new skyscraper until 1921, they were finished in 1914

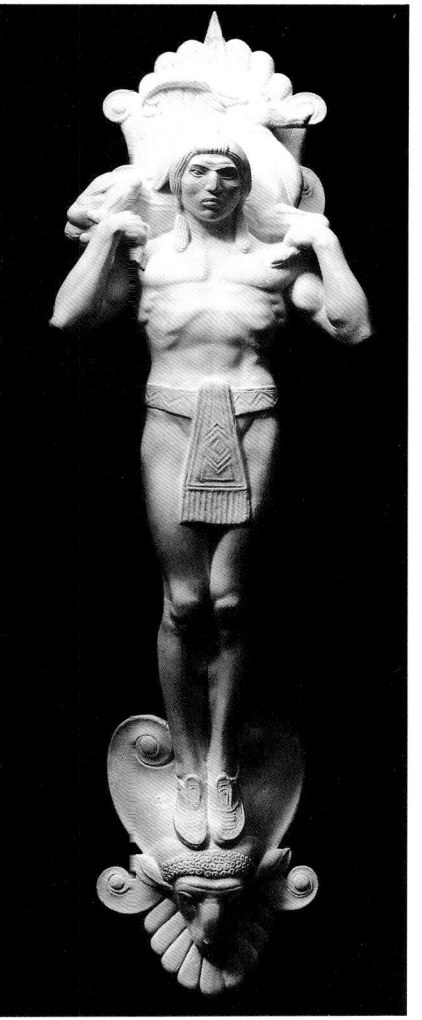

47 **DOOR PULL**, *1914*
Bronze
Designed for the
American Telephone and
Telegraph Company
Building, New York

48 **FLOOR PLAQUE**, *1914*
Bronze
Designed for the
American Telephone and
Telegraph Company
Building, New York

49 **FOUR ELEMENTS:
EARTH**, *1914*
Detail of plate 53

50 **FOUR ELEMENTS: FIRE**,
1914
Plaster

51 **FOUR ELEMENTS:
WATER**, *1914*
Plaster

52 **FOUR ELEMENTS: AIR,**
1914
Plaster

53 **FOUR ELEMENTS:**
EARTH, *1914*
Plaster

and pictured in *Vanity Fair* that September. They represent an important new direction in Manship's art. During the previous two years he had been influenced by his study of archaic Greek and Renaissance sculpture, but the rich overall treatment of these panels is certainly not classical. He looked to Chinese art for his inspiration, suggested in the highly ornamental convolutions of clouds and water, plants and flames. The four reliefs graced one of New York's busiest corners for sixty-five years, but now that the American Telephone and Telegraph Company has left its elegant Bosworth building for the new Philip Johnson tower uptown, the *Four Elements* panels are to be donated to a museum.

The desire to reproduce the effects of the great public buildings, houses, and gardens of Europe was at its height in America during the early twentieth century. The self-made American millionaire wanted gardens on a par with those of Versailles or the Boboli Gardens of the Medici, and architects like Bosworth and Charles Adams Platt were ready to supply them. Platt, in particular, was known for his country homes and gardens. He was on the board of the American Academy in Rome and had been familiar with Manship's work almost from the beginning. In 1914 he ordered a dozen terminal figures from Greek mythology (plate 54) for the garden of Harold McCormick (head of International Harvester) in Lake Forest, outside Chicago. Thus began a long series of commissions for garden sculptures, which in the next few years were to occupy much of Manship's time. By the mid-1920s, however, demand for such work had declined, perhaps because Manship's prices had gotten too high or perhaps because the very rich, with the increasing impact of income taxes, had less money to spend; but probably simply because fashions had changed. The trend in garden design shifted from the formal classicism of Renaissance Italy and prerevolutionary France to a more informal style in which there was little need for statuary.

In July 1914 the Manships—including baby Pauline—embarked for Italy

54 **CALYPSO**, *1014*
Marble, heroic size

on the German steamship *Moltke*. They were accompanied by Barry Faulkner, who was now established in a studio on MacDougal Alley. Isabel's father, David McIlwaine, had died that spring and she was now free to go abroad. War clouds were gathering in Europe, and war was declared while they were in Italy, but since Italy was to remain neutral until the following year, their traveling and sight-seeing were not much affected. They went to Milan, Venice, and Sicily and stayed a full month in Rome. The new building for the American Academy was under construction on the Janiculum. During this time Manship modeled a fountain figure of the infant Hercules

strangling a serpent (plate 55), to be placed in the courtyard of the new building as his gift. The travelers returned to New York in September on the *Europa*.

Manship was steadily building one of the busiest sculpture studios in New York, and he employed the young Italian-American sculptor Beniamino Bufano as his first assistant. A new job was the execution of two heroic-size groups, *Music* and *Dance* (plate 56), for the Panama-Pacific Exposition to be held in San Francisco in 1915. Music was exemplified by two partially draped male figures, one holding a lyre and the other, a scroll; *Dance* depicted two young women dressed in classical peplums. The groups were awarded a gold medal at the exposition. Manship sent Bufano to San Francisco to enlarge the groups from his models, and Bufano stayed on to make his reputation there.

At the same time that he was so busy in the studio, Manship was constantly exhibiting his work as well. In March 1914 he had shown a group of bronzes at the Milwaukee Art Society and at the Minnesota State Art Society in Saint Paul. The next month he had a one-man show at the Women's Cosmopolitan Club in New York, for which he received excellent press coverage. Royal Cortissoz wrote in the *New York Tribune* (May 8, 1914): "two things . . . more than any others make his sculpture fascinating, his pure, supple, really moving line, and his curious note of beauty. His linear charm would by itself give him a place apart. . . . " Cortissoz, a leading New York art critic, had not been completely enthusiastic about Manship's work in the past, but in this review he hit upon the characteristic that set Manship apart from other sculptors: his use of linear rhythms. In reviewing a show at the Architectural League the following year, Charles H. Caffin said of Manship in the *New York American* (February 9, 1915), "his work has that indefinable distinction one calls style," and he remarked that other sculptors were already imitating it. In February 1915 Manship had a show with the Pennsylvania landscape painter Richard Blossom Farley at the Saint Botolph Club in Boston, and it opened many doors in Boston and Cambridge society.

A traveling show of Manship's work was put together in 1915—extraordinary for an artist still in his twenties. It began its tour on March 15 at the Carnegie Institute's Museum of Art in Pittsburgh, and for more than a year it toured nine of the country's leading museums. Thirty-eight pieces were on exhibit at the opening, including the small bronzes that had been shown so successfully in New York, the *Infant Hercules Fountain,* the *Four Elements* reliefs, some medals, and four plasters of the figures for Harold McCormick's garden. Along the way other works were added, and the show's final stop was in Milwaukee, opening on May 1, 1916. Each museum published an attractive catalog, and the press coverage everywhere was enthusiastic and extensive.

At the same time, a collection of Manship's works was being shown in San Francisco at the Panama-Pacific Exposition, and during the summer of 1916 other selections were on view in Newport, Rhode Island, and Bar Harbor, Maine. The Bar Harbor catalog contained a short essay by Albert Eugene Gallatin that was the nucleus of the first book on Manship's work, *Paul Manship: A Critical Essay on His Sculpture, and an Iconography.* Published in New York by John Lane in 1917, this is a slight volume of fifteen pages with eight illustrations, attractively designed and bound. Gallatin was later to become an apostle of a more radical art, with his Museum of Living Art at New York University; in this text he praised Manship's work, but he urged him to produce works "even more creative and original and rather more modern in feeling."

56 **DANCE**, *1014*
Plaster, heroic size
Destroyed

This extensive series of exhibitions included a memorable show in New York at the gallery of the Berlin Photographic Company, a German dealer in photographic reproductions of well-known paintings. They owned the North American rights to *September Morn*, by the French artist Paul Chabas, and were having a phenomenal success with it. The manager of the gallery, Martin Birnbaum, an interesting and cultivated man, was one of the art world's great salesmen. To enliven the business of selling reproductions, he had begun holding one-man shows at his handsome gallery at 305 Madison Avenue. Here he had introduced to New York the works of such now-celebrated artists as Aubrey Beardsley, Léon Bakst, Elie Nadelman, and Maurice Sterne. He had a discerning eye and exquisite taste, and the list of artists he handled in six years with the Berlin Photographic Company is remarkable. In his book *Introductions,* Birnbaum cites as one of his greatest successes the exhibition of Paul Manship's sculptures.[8]

The show opened on February 15, 1916. It included the small bronzes that Paul had brought back from Rome, plus *Pauline Frances—Three Weeks Old* and the *Infant Hercules Fountain.* A number of new pieces that were to become well known and showed Manship at the top of his style and talent were also included: *Flight of Night* (plate 57), *Dancer and Gazelles* (plate 65), *Day and the Hours— Sundial* (plate 59), *Salomé* (plate 58), *Briseis, Wrestlers,* a small crucifix made for Saint John's Episcopal Church in Newport, and a group of sketches for a figure of David and for a young male hunter. This astonishing group of new pieces shows how hard the sculptor must have been working during this time. There were forty-four items in the show, ten of which were not for sale. Orders were taken for ninety pieces, meaning that many of the individual pieces were sold

57 **FLIGHT OF NIGHT**,
1916
Bronze, height: 14⅛ in.
Wadsworth Atheneum,
Hartford, Connecticut;
Gift of Philip L. Goodwin

58 **SALOME**, *1015*
Bronze, 10 x 13⅝ x
10¼ in.
National Museum of
American Art,
Smithsonian Institution,
Washington, D.C.; Gift
of the Estate of Paul
Manship

several times over. Julian Alden Weir, the celebrated Impressionist painter, bought eight bronzes with some prize money he had won at the National Academy. He wrote Manship to thank him for the "joy that your work has stirred up in me." The press was generally enthusiastic, but Royal Cortissoz was still not completely so. He found a lack of heroic dimension in Manship's work, saying he might be "inclined to describe him as a kind of literary man in art, a master of all the cultures, an eclectic to whom the schools have given precisely the sort of inspiration commended by Stevenson to his 'sedulous ape.' "[19] The charge of eclecticism was a hard one for Manship to rebut. Certainly at this period there were a host of influences in his work, but he was gradually assimilating them to create his own distinctive style.

Herbert L. Pratt, who had seen Manship's small *Indian* and *Pronghorn Antelope* at the Berlin Photographic Company show, asked him to enlarge the pieces to life size for his garden in Glen Cove, Long Island (plates 60, 61). Manship recounted their agreement this way:

> [Herbert Pratt] came to see me and said, "Now, what do you think you want to charge me for these things? Don't hesitate to charge all you think you ought to have for them," which was a great encouragement, for I would have been willing to accept any modest sum. So I made them large life-size figures, with a considerable amount of work involved, probably two years. I would have been delighted to do them for $5000 at that time. So he said, "Now, you just tell me what you think would be a nice comfortable figure for these."
>
> "Well," I said, "do you think $15,000 would be too much to ask for them?"
>
> "No," he said. "That's just right. That's fine."
>
> So I thought that was a very encouraging way to treat a young sculptor. It meant that I really was free to do the best I could and add a little surplus possibly to keep me from worrying about the next turn of the wheel.[20]

After John Pierpont Morgan died in Rome in 1913, a proposal was made almost immediately to erect a sculptured memorial tablet in New York's Metropolitan Museum of Art, of which he had been president and a major benefactor. A committee was established with Edward D. Adams as chairman, and William H. Kendall of McKim, Mead, and White, the museum's architects, drew up a plan for the memorial. Kendall approached Manship about executing the work, and in November 1915 a contract was signed between him and the Morgan Memorial Committee, for twenty thousand dollars—a major commission that was to keep Manship and his assistants occupied for five years. Finally, to crown these triumphant years, on April 26, 1916, Manship was elected to the National Academy of Design as a full Academician.

59 **DAY AND THE HOURS —SUNDIAL**, *1916*
Bronze, height: 20½ in.; diameter of base: 18 in.

60 **INDIAN**, *1017*
Bronze, 50 x 70 in.
Mead Art Museum,
Amherst College,
Amherst, Massachusetts;
Bequest of Herbert L.
Pratt

61 **PRONGHORN
ANTELOPE**, *1917*
Bronze, 35 x 50 in.
Mead Art Museum,
Amherst College,
Amherst, Massachusetts;
Bequest of Herbert L.
Pratt

5 · WASHINGTON MEWS AND CORNISH

Washington Mews is a street in Manhattan that runs just one block, from Fifth Avenue east to University Place, one block north of Washington Square. It is a row of carriage houses that served the elegant homes on the square. By the time the Manships moved there in 1915, the carriage houses had been converted into homes, and the Manships rented two of them—one as a studio (number 42) and the other as living quarters (number 44). At that time, the area north of Washington Square was popular with artists and constituted a kind of New York bohemia. The Manships were happy there, and living and working in adjoining buildings allowed Paul's time to be used even more productively.

Gaston Lachaise started working for Manship in 1916. He was a great sculptor and, because of his academic training in Paris, he was an admirable assistant as well. His only failing was a constant need for money to satisfy the expensive tastes of Isabel Nagle, his muse and obsession. When they were married, the Manships gave them their wedding party. Paul used to say, only half-jokingly, that he left New York to get away from Lachaise, who was so much in debt to him that he could never be repaid. Another man who worked in Manship's studio at this time was Reuben Nakian, still in his teens. Manship was to play something of the role in Nakian's life that Solon Borglum had played in his own, and despite the wide divergence of their art, Nakian was always to speak glowingly of Manship. In his old age he said that having been with Manship was like having worked with Michelangelo. Luigi D'Olivo, called Gigi, was the studio's general repairman and tinkerer during the Washington Mews years and on Seventy-second Street later on. He was a skilled cabinetmaker who followed Manship's designs to create several pieces of furniture that were carved by Lachaise.

Paul's relations with his family were per force conducted by mail. He wrote the news of his marriage to his sister Mary in June 1913, but she had evidently already heard about it, and her answer is filled with her hurt feelings: "Your

62 **FLIGHT OF EUROPA— ASHTRAY**, *1917*
Bronze, diameter: 2½ in.

letter came a few days ago and I was certainly glad—because I was sure I had been entirely forgotten." All her life she looked upon Paul in the proprietary way of an older sister. "My little brother," she called him, and her letters show her pride in his achievement and her affection, but also her quickness to take offense when she felt that Paul hadn't paid sufficient attention to her. Isabel never liked her very much, nor probably did Mary like Isabel. There was certainly some jealousy in their relations.

In May 1915 Paul's brother Albert turned up in New York with the manuscript of his long philosophical poem, *The Ancient of Atlantis*. He was trying to find a publisher, but this was proving to be a hard task. The poem is Whitmanesque in the worst sense—verbose and windy—but Albert, who had great confidence in his own genius, convinced Paul that he should pay to publish it. In return he turned over the copyright to Paul, but of course no royalties ever materialized and Paul never again saw the $426 he had paid to the publishers Sherman, French & Co. of Boston.

Albert must have told his brother Luther about his visit to New York, causing the family to realize that Paul's success was financial as well as artistic. They called on him for help, especially for Luther, who was the brother most seriously afflicted by bronchial asthma, the hereditary disease from which they all suffered; he was unable to work or even to lie down, and for months he hadn't had a proper night's sleep. Paul sent him money, enough for Luther to write in astonished thanks, "Anything like such generosity on your part was something I never dreamed of—and did not ever think that you were in a position to deliberately give away so much all in a bunch."

The Manships were a prosperous young couple, socially on the rise, and their home and studio were ideal for entertaining. There were some memorable parties at Washington Mews, such as the one where Charlie Chaplin and Jack Dempsey shadowboxed on the studio table. Manship was working hard, but he was also playing hard. He had joined a number of clubs: the National Arts Club; the Players Club; the Coffee House, organized by his friend Frank Crowninshield; and, his favorite, the Century Club.

The major ongoing work in Manship's studio was the Morgan tablet for the Metropolitan Museum of Art, which wasn't finished until after the war. It brought about an encounter that was to be of major importance to Paul. One of McKim, Mead, and White's young associate architects, Eric Gugler, was given the job of working with Manship on the memorial tablet. Gugler was a German-American from Milwaukee, and his character consisted of somewhat contradic-

tory elements. Although he was to conduct a successful architectural practice for more than fifty years, in many respects he was extremely impractical. He could fire up his host of friends with enthusiasm for his various projects, but despite his hard work and public-relations genius, many of these projects never got off the ground. They were often too ambitious for pragmatic Americans, who rarely thought beauty worth investing in, and Gugler may have discouraged the money men with his refusal to believe that money was as important as art. He was a classicist and an idealist, but he was also a kind of all-American bad boy, with a taste for practical jokes and high jinks. He was like a Palladio reborn as an overgrown Huck Finn. One of his favorite jokes was to place a life-size female mannequin on the toilet to see the consternation of those who walked in on her. He and Paul hit it off at once. They shared artistic idealism and a love of Italy and Greece, as well as a taste for merrymaking, bourbon, Chianti, and Havana cigars. Gugler was henceforth to be, with Barry Faulkner, Paul's closest friend.

One of Manship's favorite stories from the Washington Mews days hinged on the narrowness of the street and the pretensions of one of his *nouveau riche* clients. Welles Bosworth was the architect of the lawyer Samuel Untermyer's estate in Yonkers, New York. Bosworth wanted to place a pair of sphinxes at the entrance to a garden theater on the property. Untermyer was initially cool to the idea, fearing the expense, but he agreed to pay up to twenty-five hundred dollars. Manship accepted this price—half of what he had asked—because he knew he could make the models half-size and have the carvers enlarge them. Since the sphinxes were to be a symmetrical pair, he could also make two identical casts and just reverse the head on one of them. When the two scale models were done in plaster, Mr. and Mrs. Untermyer were invited to the studio to view them. Promptly at nine on the appointed morning a large Rolls-Royce rolled into the Mews. Mr. Untermyer got out and asked whether his wife had arrived. At that point another large Rolls-Royce drove in, and their daughter alighted. A moment later a *third* Rolls-Royce squeezed into the narrow street, to the great interest of the neighbors, and there at last was Mrs. Untermyer. They all went into the studio to look at the sculptures, and Mrs. Untermyer pointed to the one on the right. "I prefer this one," she said. "But you're to have both of them," Paul replied. "They're not the same size," Mr. Untermyer complained. Manship was so amused by the whole farce that he thought he'd play along. While protesting that they *were* the same size (knowing they had come out of the same mold), he took a pair of calipers and, letting them slip a bit, cried, "What an eye you have! I would have sworn that they were the same, but you saw this small difference. However, I can easily correct it." Mr. Untermyer was so pleased with his own astuteness that he sat down and wrote out a check for the balance he owed. When Bosworth was told the story, he said, "That's astonishing . . . the usual procedure is to have to sue him for one's money." John D. Rockefeller, when told this story, said that his old adversary Untermyer was "a very stupid man."

In the summer of 1915, with the war raging, the Manships could not go to Europe, so they followed Barry Faulkner's lead and rented a house in Cornish, New Hampshire, a small town on the Connecticut River across from Windsor,

Vermont. Augustus Saint-Gaudens had discovered it after being diagnosed as mortally ill with cancer; Barry had worked there as his assistant and had grown to like the place. Saint-Gaudens's presence had attracted other artists as well: Stephen Parrish and his son Maxfield, Charles Adams Platt, Kenyon Cox and his son Allyn, Thomas Wilmer Dewing, and others.

The Manships liked their rented house—dubbed "Mellakunk Lodge" after baby Pauline's reference to the family of skunks that lived nearby—and returned for the next two summers. Manship became closely associated with the Cornish art colony and exhibited three bronzes in a 1916 show of Cornish artists held at Dartmouth College. A number of their friends visited them in Cornish, including Martin Birnbaum, Isabel's sisters Alice and Jeannette, and Paul's assistants Lachaise and Nakian, who spent the summer of 1916 with them.

In 1916 Manship began a series of portrait medals of his artist friends. Starting with Barry Faulkner, he established the pattern for the series: on the obverse is the subject's head in profile, modeled in low relief; on the reverse is an allegory that relates to the subject's art. The reverse of the Isidore Konti medal shows an older man leading a boy, with the inscription "Guide, Philosopher, and Friend," a clear statement of Manship's relationship to the older sculptor. On the reverse of the Maxfield Parrish medal is the winged horse Pegasus, which was a symbol in Manship's oeuvre for artistic inspiration. The series was continued with medals of John Singer Sargent (plate 64), Charles Adams Platt, Welles Bosworth, and Edward Robinson.

Maxfield Parrish, who always had a penchant for mechanical things, was one of the first people in the Cornish community to own a car. In the summer of 1915 he took Manship and Faulkner on an extended trip through New Hampshire to Cape Ann, Massachusetts. This was Manship's first visit to the area that was later to be so important to him. He stopped to see the sculptor Anna Hyatt

64 **JOHN SINGER SARGENT—PORTRAIT MEDAL**, *1023*
Bronze

at her studio in Annisquam and his old teacher Charles Grafly at his studio in Lanesville. Other trips during these years included one to Bermuda in April 1916, with Isabel, Pauline, Barry, and the Platts, and several to Hewett Lake in the Adirondacks, where Sarah and Edwin Holter had a fishing lodge. The Holters, and Mrs. Holter's sister Elizabeth (Mrs. Meredith Hare), had become close friends and patrons. Manship had done garden sculpture for their estate in Mount Kisco, New York, and would later do portrait medallions of their daughters.

Through his February 1915 exhibition at the Saint Botolph Club, Manship had established contact with some of the intellectual and artistic elite of Boston, including the painter and writer Denman Ross. In May 1916 Ross wrote to Manship about an encounter he had had with John Singer Sargent. Sargent mentioned to Ross that he had been very impressed by two works in the Metropolitan Museum, but that he hadn't noticed the artist's name. When he described the artist to Ross as "the only man I know who is moved by the quest of beauty," Ross replied, "It must be Manship" and promised to arrange a meeting. He asked Paul to luncheon with Sargent on May 16. For Manship this was an event of considerable importance. Sargent was then perhaps the most celebrated painter in the world—certainly in the Anglo-American world—and his great reputation was equaled by a great generosity. He and Manship soon developed a close rapport, despite the thirty-year difference in their ages, and over the years he proved a good friend to the sculptor. Sargent wanted a small copy made of a Michelangelo and asked Manship to take care of it. Manship got Lachaise to do it, and Sargent was very pleased with the results. In December he invited Manship to join him for dinner at the Saint Botolph Club and afterwards took him over to the Boston Public Library to show him his murals. One day in 1919, while visiting at Washington Mews, Sargent asked Manship for a piece of paper. Manship told him rather casually that there was some near his hand, so Sargent made a bold and brilliant drawing of Paul on a sheet of brown wrapping paper. Pauline reported that he drew the picture as easily as he would sign his name.

Other Bostonians that Manship got to know included Thomas Whittemore, the great archaeologist, who inspired Manship with his passion for Byzantine art; Langdon Warner, the Orientalist and Harvard professor, who suggested traveling together to Japan and tried to arrange an exhibition of Manship's sculpture in Tokyo (the Manships took this seriously enough to spend a winter studying Japanese); and Paul Sachs, the art historian and curator at the Fogg Museum. Sachs bought the *Dancer and Gazelles* (plate 65) and the last available cast of the

65 **DANCER AND GAZELLES**, *1916*
Bronze, height: 32¼ in.;
base: 33 x 10 in.
The Metropolitan Museum of Art, New York; Francis Lathrop Bequest Fund, 1050

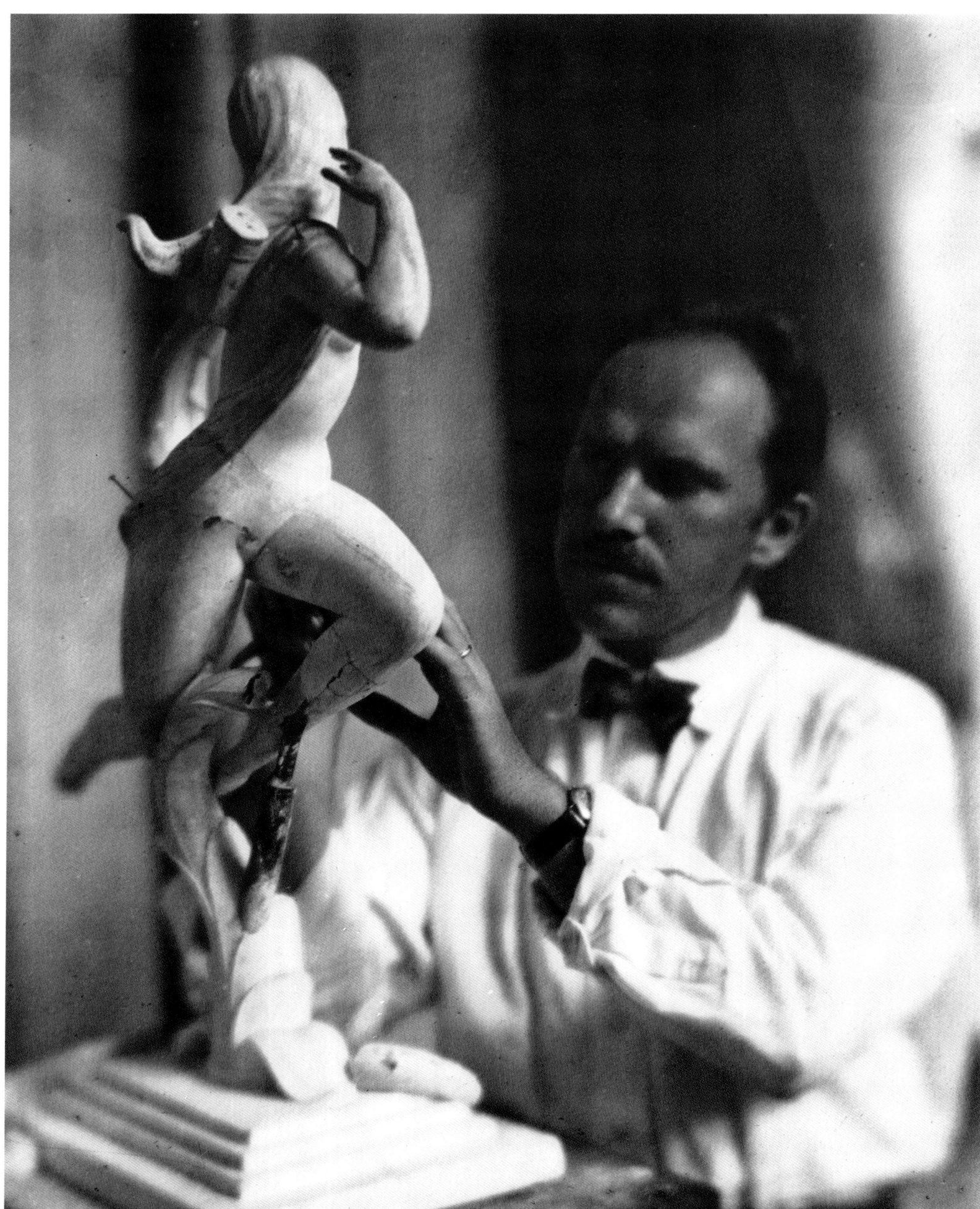

Centaur and Dryad (plate 37) for his personal collection, with the expectation that the pieces would eventually be placed in the Fogg. He wrote to Manship, "among living Americans there is no sculptor whose work interests me as much as yours does."

The queen of Boston society at that time was Isabella Stewart Gardner. Paul probably got to know her through Denman Ross, who was in her circle of intimate friends. Manship presented her with one of his Jeanne d'Arc medals (made to benefit the Italian War Relief committee; plate 67), and Mrs. Gardner

66 *Paul Manship working on* Diana, *1920*

67 **JEANNE D'ARC— MEDAL**, *1915*
Bronze, diameter: 2⅞ in.
Isabella Stewart Gardner
Museum, Boston

wrote him a rather gushy letter of thanks on May 15, 1917: "I carry it around with me everywhere, my 'paperweight.' Looking at it and feeling it give me so much pleasure. Oh it is too beautiful! Jeanne d'Arc is one I love and this is the best of her I know . . . I do not need a reminder of you, whom I have so near my heart. May the future bring us oftener together." No wonder Isabel was somewhat jealous of her. Isabel told of being with Manship and Sargent in Boston one evening when they spotted Mrs. Gardner and induced her to join them for dinner; never once during the course of the evening did Mrs. Gardner address a word to Isabel. Isabel described her as looking like an elderly monkey but said that when she spoke, her vivacity, intelligence, and charm made her seem almost beautiful. The two men in Isabel's party were obviously entranced by her. Mrs. Gardner bought a *Diana,* and Manship made an ashtray of the *Flight of Europa* (plate 62) for her, inspired by the great Titian painting she owned.

The Manships had entered quickly into the artistic and social life of New York, as well as of New England. Elizabeth Robinson, the formidable wife of the director of New York's Metropolitan Museum, got them into the Social Register —a matter of indifference to Paul, but pleasing to Isabel.

6 · WORLD WAR I AND AFTERMATH

The war had been raging in Europe since 1914, but not until 1917 did it directly affect Americans. The Manships were strongly for the Allies, as Isabel had spent a good part of her childhood in France, and Paul had those three magical years in Rome. In 1918 Manship sculpted the so-called *Kultur Medal* (plate 68), which became an object of controversy but a commercial success. On the obverse it depicts Kaiser Wilhelm II wearing a necklace of skulls; on the reverse, a brutish German soldier abducting a young woman. It was offered for sale for ten dollars to benefit the War Relief and sold briskly, but the art critics didn't like it. In the *American Magazine of Art* one wrote that "the artist desecrates the great gift with which he was divinely endowed."[21] From Cambridge, Massachusetts, Alice Longfellow, the poet's daughter, wrote: "I wish to make a strong protest against anything so hideous being issued in the name of Art or of America." These criticisms must have affected the sculptor, for he never again used his art so crudely to express his political passions.

Meanwhile, Manship's career was at its height, and he had a great deal of work to do. On February 10, 1917, he signed a contract for more than fifty thousand dollars with the landscape architect Charles Wellford Leavitt to create a number of sculptures for the garden of Charles Schwab in Loretto, Pennsylvania. This commission included two life-size bronze figures—a David (plate 70) and a mother and child; a bronze armillary sphere

68 **KULTUR MEDAL**, *1018*
Bronze, diameter: 2½ in.

69 **DAVID**, *1018*
Detail of plate 70

70 **DAVID**, *1018*
Bronze, height of figure:
04 in.; base: 5 x 20 x
25½ in.

71 **GRIFFINS**, *1017*
Limestone, height: 50 in.;
base: 43 x 10 in.
Brookgreen Gardens,
Murrells Inlet, South
Carolina
Photographed in their
original location, the
garden of Charles
Schwab, Loretto,
Pennsylvania

called *Hercules Upholding the World* (plate 76); four terra-cotta vases; four huge lead jars (plates 72–75); two limestone griffins (plate 71); and two marble herms. This massive amount of work would keep Manship and his assistants occupied throughout the summer of 1918. He was also slowly progressing on the Morgan memorial tablet (plate 81), modeling the sphinxes for Untermyer, and working on his *Diana* (plate 92). A busy year!

It was Sargent who arranged for Manship to do a portrait of John D. Rockefeller. Sargent had admired the portrait of baby Pauline (plate 44), and with an artist's imaginative leap, he saw that Manship could do a fine portrait of an old man. Sargent, who was himself painting a portrait of Rockefeller at the time, remarked to the philanthropist, "A sculptor called Manship ought to do a head of you." Bosworth, the architect of preference for the Rockefellers, acted as go-between, and in a short time the arrangements were made: Manship was to be

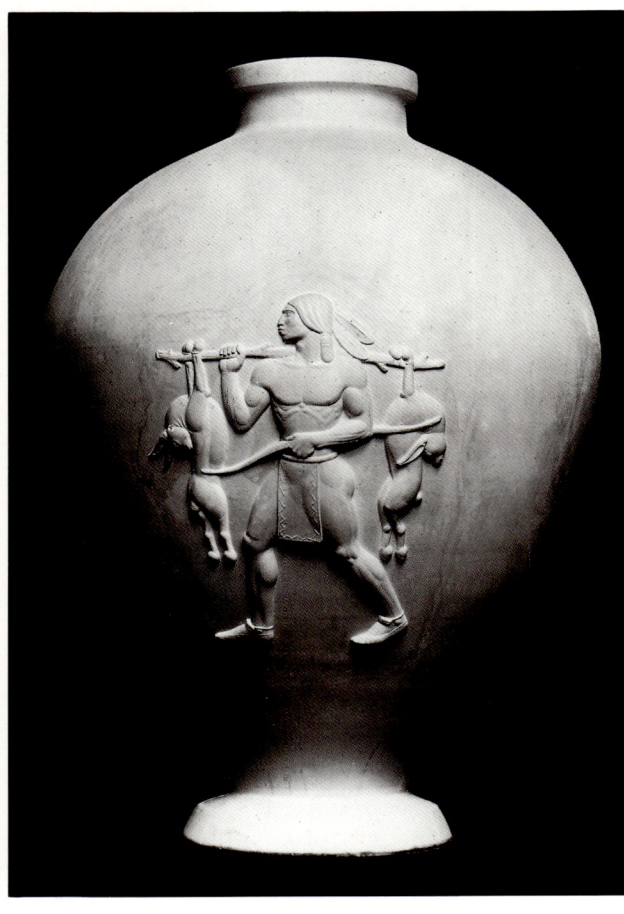

72– **FOUR VASES**, *1017*
75   *Lead, height:*
     approximately 84 in. each
     Lincoln Center,
     Minneapolis

76   **HERCULES**
     UPHOLDING THE
     WORLD—ARMILLARY
     SPHERE, *1018*
     (also known as Hercules
     Upholding the Heavens)
     Bronze, 84 x 45 in.
     Museum of Fine Arts,
     Houston; Gift of Mellie
     Esperson, Houston

paid ten thousand dollars for the marble bust, to be done largely at Pocantico—the Rockefellers' estate on the Hudson—during the summer of 1918. While Isabel and Pauline vacationed in Mattituck, Long Island, Paul stayed in New York City and drove up to Pocantico every morning. He came to admire Rockefeller, likening him to a Renaissance cardinal—hard, shrewd, intelligent, but insensitive to others in pursuit of his destiny—and his portrait shows this (plate 77). It resembles a Renaissance bust—Donatello's *Niccoló da Uzzano*, for instance—and is a remarkable accomplishment. It is Manship's first portrait of an adult and probably his best. During the same year the actor John Barrymore

77 **JOHN D. ROCKEFELLER**, *1918*
Marble, 21½ x 20 x 10½ in.

78 **JOHN BARRYMORE**, *1918*
Marble, height: 13½ in.

commissioned a portrait of himself (plate 78) as a gift for his lady friend, the poet Michael Strange (Blanche Oelrichs). The contrast with the Rockefeller bust is considerable: the crafty old millionaire and the vain and handsome actor.

When the Rockefeller portrait was done, Paul again tried to volunteer for war service. Many of his friends were in the services—Gugler, Faulkner, William Platt—but he had previously been turned down for active duty because of his chronic asthma. This time he was finally accepted as a volunteer in the American Red Cross, with the rank of lieutenant. He sailed for England in the fall of 1918, in the midst of the worldwide influenza epidemic. Thirteen people died on board, and there was a burial at sea every day. Inevitably, Paul himself came down with the disease and was very sick by the time he got to Liverpool. The doctor who tended him couldn't do much for him but did boost Manship's ego by remarking that he had read about him in the art magazines. This may have done more for the sculptor than any medicine.

On his way through London, Manship went to see Sargent, who was just back from the front and still dressed in khaki. Sargent showed him the paintings he had done in the war zone. Paul then proceeded by train to Venice, where he was to be based. The war in Italy had centered in the Veneto, and Manship was sent to a devastated region along the Piave River. He had barely arrived there, however, when the armistice was signed. The weather was dreadful, rainy and cold, and Paul, who had barely recovered from influenza, came down with pneumonia. He was sent to a hospital in Padua, where his recovery was slowed by the cold and damp, as even the hospital had no heat. When he was well enough to travel, he was sent to Rome, where he stayed at the Grand Hotel, the only one in Rome with any heat. Charles Adams Platt was there, having gone to Italy as a representative of Herbert Hoover's relief organization, as was the architect Lawrence Grant White, another Red Cross volunteer. The three of them spent the winter playing cards until a ship was available to take them back to New York. There was enough time for Manship to do a portrait medal of Platt and to design a tombstone for Frederic Crowninshield, who had died that year on Capri.

Manship's well-intentioned war service had served little purpose. He was sick almost the whole time he was in Italy, and his chronic asthma became much worse; it was to remain a serious problem for the rest of his life. This abortive experience was the first break in a Horatio Alger—style tale of steadily accelerating success, and it may have given a greater gravity to Manship's art. His work before 1918 is charming and decorative; after 1918 it relies less on charm and surface ornamentation for effect, and the sculptural forms become more powerful.

By February 1919 Manship was back in New York, where he quickly recuperated and returned to work on his numerous commissions. Lachaise had been steadily carving the Morgan tablet (plates 79–81), which was installed in the Great Hall of the Metropolitan Museum in December 1920. The museum devoted the December issue of its bulletin to the tablet, explaining its elaborate iconography. It is the most intricate of Manship's sculptures, the culmination of a tendency toward the exquisite, and it was to add Gothic art to the roster of eclectic influences on Manship's sculpture. Later his art would become simpler and more monumental.

In January 1920, the Corcoran Gallery of Art in Washington, D.C., held an exhibition of Manship's sculpture. In April, Martin Birnbaum, who was now a

partner in the firm of Scott and Fowles, exhibited Manship's marble portrait of Rockefeller in his Fifth Avenue gallery. It caused a sensation. Some critics saw it as an incisive portrayal of a greedy predator, others a sympathetic image of an old man, but all praised Manship. The critic in the *Freeman* concluded: "Nothing reveals the emptiness of success so much as this face. The Phoenicians might have placed this on the altar they raised to Mammon, the God of ill-gotten gains." The critic Peyton Boswell paid a backhanded compliment to Manship: "No one who has seen Mr. Manship's dilettante and trivial performances in imitation of the archaic Greek thought he was capable of work such as this."

79–
81 **JOHN PIERPONT
MORGAN MEMORIAL**,
1915–20
Limestone, 134 x 64 in.
The Metropolitan
Museum of Art,
New York

ERECTED·BY·THE·MUSEUM
IN·GRATEFUL·REMEMBRANCE
OF·THE·SERVICES·OF
JOHN
PIERPONT
MORGAN
FROM·1871·TO·1913
AS·TRUSTEE·BENEFACTOR
AND·PRESIDENT
HE·WAS·IN·ALL·RESPECTS
A·GREAT·CITIZEN··HE
HELPED·TO·MAKE·NEW·YORK
THE·TRUE·METROPOLIS
OF·AMERICA··HIS·INTEREST
IN·ART·WAS·LIFELONG·
HIS·GENEROUS·DEVOTION
TO·IT·COMMANDED·WORLD
·WIDE·APPRECIATION·
HIS·MUNIFICENT·GIFTS·TO
THE·MUSEUM·ARE·AMONG
ITS·CHOICEST·TREASURES

VITA·PLENA
LABORIS
M·C·M·X·X

And Royal Cortissoz wrote, "We have not in years seen so notable a work in modern sculpture."[22]

Manship continued to work on the *Diana* (plate 92) he had begun in Cornish. It represented a new departure; while still as decorative as his earlier work, it depended on the overall design and silhouette rather than on surface ornamentation for its effect. Another characteristic work, the *Cycle of Life—Armillary Sphere* (plates 82, 83), was begun at this time. It is clearly derived from *Hercules Upholding the World* (plate 76), which he had done for Schwab. Here a nuclear family is at the center, symbolic of the continuity of life within the sphere of eternity. In wartime the artist thinks about the stubborn survival of man against the odds.

In April, Paul took Isabel and Pauline south to meet his relatives. They went to Jackson, Mississippi, where the old aunts were still living in the Manship house on Fortification Street; then to Baton Rouge, Louisiana, to see his cousin Charley Manship, the successful publisher of the *State Times* and *Morning Advocate*. That summer, rather than returning to Cornish, they rented a house in Portsmouth, New Hampshire. Paul seriously considered buying a house in Portsmouth but eventually decided he had other plans for the future than settling in New England. It was old England that enticed him and France, where he had originally wanted to study. So during 1920 and the first part of 1921 he devoted himself to finishing his commissions so that he could leave New York. His excuse was an exhibition scheduled for June 1921 at the Leicester Galleries in London, which Sargent had arranged for him. In May 1921 the Manships sailed for England on the RMS *Adriatic*.

82 **CYCLE OF LIFE—
ARMILLARY SPHERE**,
1028
Bronze, diameter: 00 in.
Phillips Academy,
Andover, Massachusetts

7 · EUROPE

Isabel reported to Barry Faulkner that Paul was a little depressed at leaving New York, and even the availability of legal liquor on board didn't help much. But he really was glad to get away. He had been working very hard on commissioned pieces, and now he was free to follow his own fantasy. The family settled into an apartment on the  Thames that Sargent's sister had found for them, and Manship moved into Sargent's studio at 33 Tite Street, although Sargent him- self was in Boston.

Manship had been spoiled by the great fi- nancial success of his New York shows, and he was disappointed by the poor sales from the Leicester Galleries exhibition. Nonetheless, he was able to sell three bronzes, which was as much as could be ex- pected in an impover- ished postwar London. He wrote to Barry on July 12, 1921, "There are several kinds of so-called successes—but the kind that really convinces me is the financial kind—it's the merry, merry jingle of the cold hard cash."

Manship's friends went out of their way to introduce him to the leaders of England's social and art worlds. Sargent had written to the connoisseur Sir Philip Sassoon from America, asking him to do what he could for Manship, and Sassoon was happy to comply, calling him the "world's greatest sculptor" in a letter to Sargent written that June. Sassoon's sister, Lady Rocksavage (later the Marchioness of Cholmondeley), commissioned a portrait that was to be one of Manship's most successful portraits of a woman. The sculptor had met the Bernard Berensons the previous winter in New York, and now Mary Berenson sent him letters of introduction to a number of influential people, including Eric

MacLagan, director of the Victoria and Albert Museum; the critic Claud Phillips; the painter Sir William Rothenstein; and Bertrand Russell.

In the fall the Manships moved to Paris, where they settled in a hotel near the place de l'Étoile. Paul shared the painter Paul Dougherty's studio on the boulevard Montparnasse while he was searching for one of his own. He had completed the small *Diana* (plate 92) in New York earlier that year, and he was now working on a companion piece—*Actaeon* (plate 85). He had also finished two small bronzes, *Spear Thrower* (plate 86) and *Atalanta* (plate 87), both masterful portrayals of bodies in motion.

85 **ACTAEON**, *1022*
Bronze, 7½ x 8 in.; base: 4½ x 2¼ in.

86 **SPEAR THROWER**, *1021*
Bronze, height: 18 in.; base: 17 x 7½ in.

In October, Paul met the Berensons in Venice and drove back with them to their Tuscan villa, I Tatti. He was very friendly with Berenson during this period. In fact, the following year Berenson asked Manship to accompany them to Egypt and was quite upset when the sculptor refused, pleading that he was too busy. The friendship was interrupted, however, by a misunderstanding. Manship asked Berenson to pose for him, intending, as was his practice with his friends, to give him a copy of the portrait. Berenson replied that he would be happy to pose as long as it was clearly understood that he shouldn't be expected to pay for it. Paul was so offended that his friend Berenson would think he was one of those artists who would coerce friends into acquiring their work that he didn't see Berenson again until after World War II.

On November 15 Isabel gave birth in the Paris hotel to their second daughter, who was named Elizabeth Robinson, in honor of Mrs. Edward Robinson. As at Pauline's birth, Manship modeled a medal to commemorate the event and pre-

87 **ATALANTA**, *1021*
Bronze, height: 28¾ in. National Museum of American Art, Smithsonian Institution, Washington, D.C.; Gift of the Estate of Paul Manship

sketch for garden figure

sented it to Isabel. He also started a sculpture of the infant but didn't finish it until eight years later, when he transformed it into a marble portrait (plate 125) of his youngest daughter, Sarah Janet (always known as Sarah Jane). Elizabeth, who was nicknamed "Chou Chou," was a sickly child, and Isabel employed a governess to take care of her, Louise Portaillier, whom the children called "Tata." For the next fifteen years she was to be an important member of the Manship household.

Meanwhile, Paul was glorying in Paris. He wrote to Barry (December 30, 1921): "Paris is the center of the world—and while I am not in the center of the whirlpool I feel the motion of it"; and "My coming here is no mistake—I feel inspired to go ahead—and I hope to see my own ideas more clearly and to carry out my work in better form." He had some trouble finding a studio and admitted to Barry that he was tempted to move to Rome, where he could always use the Academy facilities. He realized that Rome "would have none of the pep which is part of the atmosphere of this town. . . . While I am a lover of antiquities, I have no desire to be an antiquarian or archeologist." He worked in various studios until 1924, when he found the perfect one. It was at 6, rue du Val de Grace, in the garden of a seventeenth-century convent originally built by Louise de La Vallière and now filled with artists' studios. Manship's was a splendid two-story structure with excellent light, large enough to accommodate any work he wanted to do. It cost only about a hundred dollars a year; no wonder he kept it until 1937, when the fear of war led him to give it up.

Manship did many portraits in Paris, which was curious for a man who had shunned Charles Grafly's portrait class in Philadelphia and who had previously done only four portraits. He modeled the American ambassador Myron Herrick, his friend Frederick Keppel, and even "America's sweetheart," Mary Pickford. He traveled back to England to execute several others, including the young Vivian St. George, whose mother he had met through the Irish painter William Orpen, who was one of Manship's frequent companions during the winter of 1921–22. The renowned art dealer Sir Joseph Duveen had arranged to have Manship do a portrait of the Prince of Wales, but the prince would agree to only two sittings. Manship found the young man physically unattractive and had no appetite for the work, especially after Sargent advised him that it would cause him nothing but headaches, so he gladly let the matter drop.

One portrait that was to lead to greater things was that of the rich American widow Grace Rainey Rogers, who went to Manship's Paris studio to pose for a statuette. Her friendship and patronage were to prove very important in subse-

88 **SKETCH FOR GARDEN FIGURE: SATYR PLAYING PIPES**, *1920s Brush and gray and black washes and pencil on cream laid paper, 7⅝ x 6¼ in. (irregular)*

quent years. A likeness that gave him a good deal of trouble was that of Dr. M. Carey Thomas (plate 89), the redoubtable president of Bryn Mawr College and a cousin of Mary Berenson. The sculptor tried three times but could not get the likeness right and was willing to admit defeat, but Dr. Thomas was made of sterner stuff. She insisted that he try again and postponed her departure for the United States; this time he was successful at last. Other portraits from this period include one of the Oriental rug collector James Ballard, which later went

with his collection to the Metropolitan Museum; two of the girl Genevieve Brady —a head and a full figure, seated with her dog; and one of Manship's daughter Elizabeth at three years of age, holding a doll. Portraits are a relatively undemanding way for an artist to earn a living, and they proved a welcome source of funds in these years when Manship had no major architectural commissions. A gregarious man, he also enjoyed the interaction with his sitters, who tended to be exceptionally interesting people.

While in Paris, Manship also did a number of portrait medallions in relief: one of each of his daughters, one of Count Boni de Castellane, and another of the critic and editor August Jaccaci. Jaccaci arranged to have Paul Vitry, the curator of sculpture at the Louvre, do a book on Manship, and he was instrumental in obtaining a commission for him to do a funerary monument for Père Lachaise Cemetery to commemorate a couple named De Bocande. The sculpture, intended to show their deep devotion to each other, was of a man and woman

seated side-by-side and holding hands (plate 90). Later Manship admitted that he was disappointed with the results and found the work rather stiff. In many ways an early study for it was more interesting, portraying an angel on its knees holding two hearts (plate 91).

The most important pieces that Manship did during these Paris years were the *Diana* and *Actaeon*. The idea for the groups went back to his second summer in Cornish, and the small *Diana* (plate 92) had been finished before his departure from New York. In 1924–25 he enlarged the *Diana* and created an *Actaeon* in the same size (plates 93, 94). These pieces represent Manship at his most characteristic, with their use of mythological subjects, nude figures in motion, stylized animals and plants, and highly decorative patterns in which the voids are as calculated for effect as the solids. These two pieces have always been—with the *Dancer and Gazelles* (plate 65)—Manship's most popular works.

Manship had been invited to serve as professor of sculpture at the American Academy in Rome for the winter of 1921–22, but he had requested that the appointment be postponed until the following year, when Barry Faulkner would be in Rome. He and Manship had been commissioned to create a war memorial for the Academy honoring its veterans—in particular, the sculptor Harry Thrasher, who had died in battle. Thrasher was a friend of Faulkner's whom Manship had met in 1912 in Rome. (Eric Gugler was also involved in the project, but Manship and Faulkner largely ignored his plans.) During the 1923 visit Paul had some work done by the Florentine founder Vignali and met his young son-in-law Bruno Bearzi, who in time was to be Paul's principal bronze founder. Manship's and Faulkner's main interest at this time was in French Romanesque art. They drove around southern France seeking out small churches with Romanesque cloisters, tympana, or frescoes. What fascinated Manship about the art of this period was what had fascinated him about that of the Greek archaic period: the simplicity of the form, the stylization of details, and the subordination of all the parts to a rhythmic design. These were qualities he was trying to incorporate into his own work.

In May 1923 Manship exhibited his sculpture for the first time in Paris, in a show designed to introduce to the French the accomplishments of certain American artists. The painters in the show were Winslow Homer, John Singer Sargent, and, surprisingly, Dodge MacKnight. During 1924 and 1925 he created the two *Europa* groups. The earlier portrays Europa nestled against the seated bull, with her hands on his horns. It was done in bronze in two sizes and also exists in marble in the larger size (plates 95–97). The second depicts the flight of Europa

92 **DIANA**, *1921*
Bronze, height: 20 in.;
base: 13½ x 7½ in.

93 **DIANA**, *1024*
Gilded bronze, height:
87 in.; base: 45 x 23½ in.
Brookgreen Gardens,
Murrells Inlet, South
Carolina

94 **ACTAEON**, *1024*
Gilded bronze, height:
85 in.; base: 45 x 24 in.
Brookgreen Gardens,
Murrells Inlet, South
Carolina

95, **EUROPA AND THE**
96 **BULL**, *1924*
   Bronze, height: 9¼ in.;
   length: 11½ in.

97 **EUROPA AND THE**
   BULL, *1920*
   Marble, height: 23 in.;
   base: 20 x 13 in.
   Private collection

98 **PLASTILENE SKETCH FOR "FLIGHT OF EUROPA,"** *early 1920s*
Destroyed

99, **FLIGHT OF EUROPA,**
100 *1925*
Bronze, 20½ x 30 in.
Brookgreen Gardens, Murrells Inlet, South Carolina
Plate 99, photographed in the artist's studio, shows the original gold-leaf patina.

(plates 99, 100): the maiden is seated backward on the bull as he races through the sea, with the god of love whispering in her ear. The pieces are marvelously stylish, with a mischievous humor evident in Manship's portrayal of the bull as a grossly exaggerated figure of masculinity.

Manship finally gave up the lease on his house and studio in Washington Mews in 1923, and it was taken over by Gaston Lachaise. From then on, whenever Manship had to go to New York on business he stayed with friends. He spent two months in 1924 with the Edward Robinsons at their house on Irving Place in New York and traveled to Palm Beach that winter. He was obviously working to maintain his network of American friends and patrons, but so many of Manship's American friends passed through Paris at this time that vital contacts were made right there. Welles Bosworth had given up his New York architectural practice and accepted a position in Paris representing John D. Rockefeller, who was subsidizing the restoration of the cathedral at Reims and the palace of Versailles. Bosworth wanted to go to Egypt, where it was proposed that a new Cairo museum be erected to his design with Rockefeller's money, so in February 1924 Bosworth, Manship, and Faulkner traveled to Egypt via Crete, where they visited the excavations at Knossos; they returned via Istanbul to see the Byzantine mosaics that Thomas Whittemore was uncovering. The sculptor Mahonri Young was often in Paris at this time, and Manship would lend him his studio whenever he was out of town. Other younger American sculptors Manship came to know in Paris included Nathaniel Choate, Donald Delue, George Demetrios (who was a student of the French artist Emile-Antoine Bourdelle), Wheeler Williams, and Walker Hancock, the latter two being Fellows of the Rome Academy. The painters Paul Dougherty and Leon Kroll were good friends who often traveled with the Manships to see old churches and Romanesque carvings.

Manship saw a good deal of his friend Hunt Diederich, who was also living in Paris. More than with any other sculptor, Paul saw eye-to-eye with Hunt, although Diederich maintained closer ties to the avant-garde than Manship. On one occasion Diederich took him to Constantin Brancusi's studio. Manship admired the material qualities of Brancusi's work—the polish and finish of the metal or stone—but otherwise did not see much in it. But he came to Brancusi's defense a few years later after U.S. Customs officials refused to accept one of Brancusi's sculptures as art and therefore charged duty on it. In the ensuing trial Manship was one of the sculptors who testified that this work, though abstract, was indeed art of high quality.

In April 1925 the *Exposition Internationale des Arts Décoratifs et Industriels Modernes* opened at the Grand Palais and in various pavilions constructed for the occasion along the Seine. This exhibition has since assumed nearly mythic proportions in the history of art, and it has given the name Art Deco to a whole school of twentieth-century art. Manship and Janet Scudder were the only American sculptors represented in the show. Manship exhibited his *Cycle of Life* (plate 82) in the Grand Palais in the section devoted to garden sculpture. Isabel reported to Barry Faulkner that she and Paul had visited the show many times and found it "more than interesting, full of ideas." Manship's work, especially *Diana* and *Actaeon*, was now closer to the Art Deco stereotype, but he was always offended at being labeled an Art Deco

sculptor. He understood the term to refer to certain commercially fabricated decorative pieces being made then, but in the broader sense of a general movement characterized by sleek modernity and high stylization of natural forms, the term Art Deco does apply to Manship's work of this period.

Harriet Beale, a friend of the Manships, wanted a monument created in memory of her son, who had been killed in the war in France. She had purchased a plot of land in the village where he had fallen and had gotten permission from the village council to erect a monument there. She asked Manship to create the sculpture, and he modeled a life-size figure of a young man in uniform, standing in front of a cross (plate 102). A contract to have the work carved in limestone had already been signed when General John J. Pershing, who was chairman of the Battle Monuments Commission, happened to visit Manship's studio about another matter: an urn that Manship was making for the American Military Cemetery at Thiaucourt, France. Pershing asked about the statue of the soldier and, when told of Mrs. Beale's plan, informed Manship that private monuments

to the war dead were absolutely forbidden. Things seemed to be at an impasse until Manship discovered that the general knew Mrs. Beale, who was a daughter of the Republican senator from Maine, James G. Blaine, and a sister of Mrs. Walter Damrosch. The solution was to erect the Beale monument at Thiaucourt, where it still stands, a handsome image of a young American who had died fighting in Europe (plate 101).

In January 1925 Manship returned to New York for eight months. He had left the city because he was tired, perhaps of too much success or at least of too many demands on his time. In Paris he had entered the mainstream of contemporary art and developed a kind of sculptural design that was typically his own, exemplified by *Diana* and *Actaeon*, the two *Europa* groups, *Atalanta*, *Adam* and *Eve* (plate 103), and *Spear Thrower*. His ambition now, perhaps whetted by the Thiaucourt statue, was to create major public monuments. To do this he had to go back to New York.

103 **ADAM** *and* **EVE**, *1025*
Bronze, height: 17½ in.
and 10 in., respectively;
bases: 4⅝ x 4⅝ in. each

104 **VENUS**
ANADYOMENE
FOUNTAIN, *1027*
Marble, height: 77½ in.;
diameter of base: 05 in.
Addison Gallery of
American Art, Phillips
Academy, Andover,
Massachusetts

8 · THE MAJOR WORKS

It was probably in 1924 in Paris, while posing for her portrait figurine, that Grace Rainey Rogers asked Manship whether he would be interested in creating a memorial to her brother to be erected at the Bronx Zoo. Paul Rainey had been a big-game hunter and animal collector who had trapped rare animals for the zoo until his death the previous year. After a few other ideas (plate 108), Manship proposed a set of mon-  umental bronze gates. For him it was a dream commission, the chance to do something en- tirely new—an archi- tectural structure in sculpture. He would be modeling animals, at which he excelled, and best of all, there would be no committees look- ing over his shoulder. Mrs. Rogers would give him free rein, plenty of money, and no dead- line. On his return to New York in January 1925 he worked out the details with Mrs. Rogers and, on the strength of her commitment, he looked around for a house to buy.

Isabel often said that her husband overdid things. She had remarked that she would like to own a home in New York, so Manship bought not one house, but five: four brownstone tenements on East Seventy-second Street and one on East Seventy-third. To finance this deal he borrowed thirty thousand dollars from Mrs. Rogers in an agreement, signed on July 3, 1925, that called for the money to be repaid by his work on the gates. He asked Eric Gugler to prepare plans to renovate two of the houses, 319 and 321 East Seventy-second Street, and left the other three as they were. In the backyard of 319 he built his studio. The house itself was done over in palatial style for his family, with the top floor designed as a studio apartment for Barry Faulkner. The building next door was divided into three apartments and two artists' studios in order to suit the needs of several of the Manships' friends: the ground-floor garden apartment was

114

intended for the music critic Richard Stokes and his wife; the large duplex on the second floor was for Riccardo Bertelli (the president of the Roman Bronze Foundry) and his family; and the smaller duplex in the rear was for Isabel's sister Jeannette, her husband Leonard Stanley, and her niece Cornelia Hopkins, who had been living with them since her parents' death. One of the top-floor studios was used by Albert (Bertie) Gallatin (cousin of A. E. Gallatin), who was an enthusiastic Sunday painter. Renovations progressed slowly, and it wasn't until December 1926 that the Manships were able to move in. Meanwhile, Paul had a lot of thinking to do about the gates and other projects coming his way.

In the optimistic spirit of the late 1920s, the banker Thomas Cochran was spending huge sums of money on various building projects that interested him. He was largely responsible for funding the reconstruction of the campus of his old school, Phillips Academy, in Andover, Massachusetts. The architect was Charles Adams Platt, who had introduced Cochran to Manship in Paris, where Paul did his portrait. They asked Manship to design an armillary sphere as a central point of the campus. The idea was that an open sphere would not block the view down the central axis of Platt's design. Manship developed his *Cycle of Life—Armillary Sphere* (plate 82) to heroic scale, but then Platt decided that the sphere should be placed off-center, to the right of the central axis, where it now stands. To balance it, Manship proposed a celestial sphere for the left side, but Cochran rejected the idea, most likely feeling that he was already spending enough money.

Cochran did have another commission for Manship: a fountain for Saint Paul, to be placed in Cochran Park, near the Cochran family home. In May 1925 the artist traveled to Saint Paul, where he met Cochran's architect on the project, Magnus Jemne. Together they studied the site and determined the details of the design. Manship proposed a life-size figure of an Indian running with a dog at his side; it was to be set up in the center of a pool, encircled by four Canada geese spouting water through their mouths. Manship had been doing sculptures of Indians, hunters, or Davids—partially nude young men with dogs at their sides—for over ten years, beginning with *Spirit of the Chase* (plate 43) for Harold L. Pratt. His habit was to keep working at a theme until he got it right, and *Indian Hunter and His Dog* for Saint Paul was the culmination of this sequence. The small version (plate 107) has always been one of his most popular pieces. The original was moved to Saint Paul's Como Park in the 1960s, after a newspaper campaign pointed out the vandalism the fountain had suffered in Cochran Park. Eventually a fiberglass copy was installed at the original site.

While in Saint Paul, Manship took the opportunity of seeing many of his old friends and relatives. It was now almost sixteen years since his last visit. He particularly wanted to see his brother Luther, whom he found so weakened by asthma that he was at best able to sit in a wheelchair. Paul suggested that he move to a warm climate and pledged two hundred dollars a month to support Luther and his wife in Southern California. There Luther showed considerable improvement and was able to return to painting. He was, however, to remain financially dependent on Paul until Luther's death in 1931.

107 **INDIAN HUNTER AND HIS DOG**, *1926*
Bronze, 20³/₄ x 24 in.;
base: 12¹/₂ x 6 in.

When he returned to New York, Manship found the new studio was not yet ready, so he went back to Paris at the beginning of August to work on the *Indian Hunter and His Dog*. He stopped in Brussels to inspect the Compagnie des Bronzes, which he decided to have cast the Bronx Zoo gates. By December he was back in New York, and this time the studio, at least, was almost ready. In January 1926 he started writing letters under the address 319 East Seventy-second Street, as he would for almost thirty years.

Whenever he had a major project to do, Manship took an approach rather like a lawyer's: he checked the precedents. In the case of the gates for the Bronx Zoo, he knew that most monumental gates of the past had been made of wrought iron and that the great masters of ironwork had been the Spanish. He therefore resolved to go to Spain and arranged a driving trip for the spring of 1926 with Isabel, their friend Mrs. Kellogg Fairbank of Chicago, and her daughter Janet. The party left Paris and traveled slowly to Madrid, stopping in Burgos, Toledo, Avila, and the other cities of Castile, where Manship could study the great iron grilles in the cathedrals.

He made many drawings for the gates (plates 109, 110) but was unable to reconcile their large scale with the delicacy of wrought iron; he eventually decided in favor of bronze. His early drawings feature a figure of Orpheus in the center of the composition—no doubt because Orpheus, the divine musician, was able to charm animals by the power of his music—but this mythological element was ultimately dropped. The finished gates (plates 111, 112) are centered on a lion, balanced by a leopard and a baboon, with bears and deer in the spandrels above the openings, birds in the ornamental vegetation of the frame, and the whole resting on the backs of three turtles. The modeling of the animals was largely done in a special studio set aside for Manship at the zoo, where the animals were taken for him to study. Then he proceeded to design the frame, with its stylized plant forms, and finally the gatehouses, which Platt's office helped him with. It was eight years before all the work was finished.

The Manships returned to New York in December 1926 to set up residence in the newly refurbished house at 319 East Seventy-second Street. Isabel was pregnant again, and after several miscarriages she was being very careful. She said she was eager to get back home so that her son would not have to serve in the French army when he came of age. She was certain that after two girls she would have a boy, and indeed she was right. Their son, born on January 16, 1927, was named John Paul for John Singer Sargent and for his father.

As though the work on the zoo gates and the Cochran commissions weren't

108 **STUDY FOR MONUMENT: EQUESTRIAN FIGURE ON A COLUMN**, *n.d. Pencil on cream tracing paper, 14⅞ x 5 in. (irregular) Minnesota Museum of Art, Saint Paul; Bequest of the Estate of Paul Howard Manship*

109 STUDY FOR BRONX ZOO GATE, *c. 1920–34*
Pen and black ink over pencil on tan tracing paper, 8½ x 25¾ in. Minnesota Museum of Art, Saint Paul; Bequest of the Estate of Paul Howard Manship

110 SKETCH FOR PAUL J. RAINEY MEMORIAL GATEWAY, *1920*
Ink and pencil on paper

Pages 120–21
111, PAUL J. RAINEY
112 MEMORIAL GATEWAY, *1934*
Bronze, 30 x 42 ft. New York Zoological Park, Bronx

Pages 122–23
113 GROUP OF BIRDS: CROWNED CRANE, CONCAVE-CASQUED HORNBILL, BLACK-NECKED STORK, GOLIATH HERON, FLAMINGO (#1), *and* **PELICAN** *(from left), 1932*
Gilded bronze on lapis lazuli bases, height: 9⅝ to 10¼ in. National Museum of American Art, Smithsonian Institution, Washington, D.C.; Gift of the Estate of Paul Manship

114 *Paul Manship working on*
Abraham Lincoln—the
Hoosier Youth, *1020*

enough to keep him busy, Manship accepted three other major commissions in the next few years. In 1927 the architect Benjamin Morse, who was designing the headquarters of the Lincoln Life Insurance Company in Fort Wayne, Indiana, asked Manship to model a statue of Abraham Lincoln to be placed in front of the building. Manship took a three-dimensional sketch (plate 115) to Fort Wayne to discuss the details of the commission with the company's officers; while there he also set up a cardboard cutout of the statue at the site to test the scale and determined that twice life-size would be right.

Prior to the meeting Manship had decided to charge thirty-five thousand dollars for the statue, but when the president of the company showed him a list of what other sculptors had been paid for statues of Lincoln, he realized that he could double that amount and still be within range. A contract was signed for seventy-five thousand dollars for the bronze statue, exclusive of the pedestal. Certain changes in the sketch were required—specifically in the clothing, to make it more historically accurate, and in the breed of dog, which was to be an Ohio River hound. Manship was able to borrow a bitch of this breed from a friend in Kentucky, and he took her to Paris to serve as a model. The dog, Firefly, was much beloved of the Manship children during her summer residence. Manship steeped himself in Lincoln lore, reading half a dozen books and traveling with the insurance company historian through southern Indiana and Kentucky, where Lincoln had grown up.[23] Manship's statue (plate 114) was finally dedicated in an elaborate day-long ceremony on September 16, 1932, with speeches by various political personages and historians.[24]

In 1926 Manship was invited to participate in an international competition to design coinage for the Irish Free State. William Butler Yeats had inspired this

115 **PLASTILENE SKETCH FOR "ABRAHAM LINCOLN—THE HOOSIER YOUTH,"** *1020*

competition and selected the motifs for the designs, which were the animals most associated with Irish life: the horse, the hound, the hen, the salmon, the bull, the hare, the ram, and the woodcock—with a harp on the reverse. Manship rarely entered competitions, but this one interested him enough to do several models (plates 116–23). His fellow competitors included some of the most distinguished sculptors then at work, such as Ivan Meštrovič and Carl Milles; but the jury selected the entries of the English sculptor Percy Metcalf. Manship later admitted that had he been a juror he would have made the same choice, and the Irish coins are indeed unusually handsome.

116– **DESIGNS FOR THE**
123 **COINAGE OF THE**
IRISH FREE STATE,
1027
John and Margaret
Manship

Early in 1929 Manship was commissioned to make a monumental equestrian statue of General Ulysses S. Grant to be placed in front of Grant's Tomb on Riverside Drive in Manhattan. The architect John Russell Pope was refurbishing the building and relandscaping the site, and the equestrian monument was the centerpiece of his plans. The project intrigued Manship because he had wanted to create an equestrian statue ever since his apprenticeship with Solon Borglum. But Manship's usual good luck seemed to fail him whenever it came to equestrian statues. The Grant's Tomb project was going well, with most of the money pledged, when the stock market crashed in October 1929. The pledges were rescinded, leaving only enough money to pay Pope for his plans and Manship for his studies (plate 124). Efforts were later made to revive the project, but none succeeded. After Manship's death, the New York Historical Commission bought the bronze casting of his preliminary study and placed it inside the tomb. So the matter was concluded.

Manship had as little luck with church sculpture as he had with equestrians.

124 **STUDY FOR "ULYSSES**
S. GRANT," *1028*
Plaster, height: 00 in.

During this period he was asked to do several sculptures for churches, but they all came to nought. Ralph Adams Cram wanted him to make a baptismal font for the Cathedral of Saint John the Divine in New York, but when Manship discovered that all that was expected of him was to execute Cram's drawing, he refused, and the work was done by Albert Atkins of Providence. The architectural firm McGinnis and Walsh likewise wanted him to make monumental bronze doors for Saint Patrick's Cathedral in New York—which excited Manship, who fervently admired the doors by Ghiberti and Bonnano da Pisa—but the Depression hit. When money became available

125 *Paul Manship with his daughter Sarah Janet and a portrait of her, 1930*

again after World War II, the work was done by John Angel. In the 1950s Manship was asked to model a grille for a chapel in the National Cathedral in Washington, D.C., but although he did a number of interesting drawings, the commission fell through.

On June 19, 1929, the Manships' last child was born at the American hospital in Paris—a little girl christened Sarah Janet in honor of the Manships' friend and patron Sarah Holter and the novelist Janet Fairbank. Isabel, who was almost forty-six years old, had always had difficult pregnancies, and serious problems this time kept her in the hospital for an extra forty days. The children were with Louise in the south of France, leaving Paul alone in his Paris studio. He was in his early forties, a notoriously restless period in a man's life, and it was during this time that he began a relationship with Lucienne, a French woman interested in art. Their involvement, which continued until at least the mid-1930s, was somewhat public: in 1934, for example, they went on a skiing trip to Gstaad with the Bosworths. Isabel found out about this relationship through a family friend, the sculptor Harold Erskine, and she was understandably upset; but she was a stoical woman who bore her grief with dignity, convinced that in the long run she would prevail, as she did. After a few years, Manship did tire of Lucienne, but what caused the final break was his discovery that a man she had introduced

126 **THESEUS AND
ARIADNE**, *1928*
*Limestone, 50½ x 82⅝ x
32⅛ in.*
*National Museum of
American Art,
Smithsonian Institution,
Washington, D.C.;
Transfer from the New
York State Parks and
Recreation Department*

as her brother was in fact another of her lovers. He last heard from her in 1940, when Lucienne (who was Jewish) wrote asking for help in leaving Paris, but there was nothing he could do for her.

What Lucienne did for Paul was to involve him in left-wing politics, for she was an active and proselytizing member of the Communist party. Manship had never been particularly interested in politics, but he, like many other men of good will, moved toward communism during the 1930s in response to the Depression and the rise of fascism. Manship never became a communist, but he gave his support to many left-wing groups. As his infatuation with Lucienne declined, however, so did his commitment to Marxist politics.

The stock-market crash of 1929 indirectly led to the creation of Manship's most celebrated sculpture, because the Depression gave birth to Rockefeller Center.[25] A committee of architects, headed by Raymond Hood, had drawn up imaginative plans calling for a pedestrian mall from Fifth Avenue to the foot of the center's main building, which was to house the Radio Corporation of America (RCA). Art was intended to play an important part in the complex. A professor of philosophy from the University of Southern California, Hartley Burr Alexander (who had previously served the architect Bertram Goodhue in the same capacity on the state capitol in Lincoln, Nebraska), was employed to work out a consistent iconography for the art to be commissioned. The theme he chose for the center was "New Frontiers and the March of Civilization." Times were bad, and the construction of such an ambitious project was a sign of faith in a prosperous future; art was to underline this message.

127 **SEA GOD**, *1930*
Bronze, 0 x 0 in.

128 **ELEMENTS—SKETCH**,
1930
Bronze, 7¼ x 5½ in.

The architects had Manship in mind from the beginning as sculptor of the key work, a fountain for the sunken plaza to be constructed at the base of the RCA Building. Various designs were proposed, one of which was for an armillary sphere similar to the one Manship had done at Andover. Manship himself wanted to create a colossal group of figures, forty feet tall, but this idea was shot down by the various committees in charge, to the sculptor's great disappointment. The reasons given were that it would take too long to create, would cost too much, and would weigh too much for the underground concourse. Manship and his assistants produced dozens of sketches of possible subjects (plates 127, 128) before the theme of Prometheus, originally suggested by Professor Alexander, was settled upon, although Manship himself was never completely happy with it.

Among the plethora of preliminary sketches are a few that fixed the subject as we know it (plate 129): the nude figure of the Titan, with a flame in his right hand, is shown flying from Mount Olympus, which is encircled by the ring of the zodiac. His theft of fire was, of course, what permitted the progress of civilization. The work was to be two-and-a-half times life-size, so Manship prepared a model about twenty-four inches long—one-eighth the final size. He and his assistants used a pantograph to make the full-size plaster copy (plate 130) directly from this model. This was a relatively quick way to do the work, as time was of the essence, bypassing the usual modeling in clay or plastilene, the mold-making, and the casting in plaster. Manship had already used this technique of direct modeling in plaster on a large scale for the figure of Lincoln, which he was finishing at the same time. He had always been praised for

his ability to meet deadlines, and he didn't disappoint his clients this time. In 1934 the statue (plate 132) was in place for the dedication of Rockefeller Center.

From the beginning *Prometheus* attracted an enormous amount of attention. In the early years of Franklin D. Roosevelt's administration the bright gold youth was said to symbolize America's going off the gold standard. The National Broadcasting Company has used it so often in their publicity that it's become a kind of unofficial logo for them. And tourists have photographed it so frequently that, next to the Statue of Liberty, it has come to be the best-known work of public art in the country. This popularity rather annoyed Paul, as he never considered *Prometheus*, which he had created in a rush against a deadline, to be his best work. Yet it is characteristic of his art: the gravity-defying figure with its stylized details, the strongly rhythmic outline of the composition, even the ring of the zodiac are all essential elements of Manship's mature work.

In the original composition there were two groups placed on either side of the main sculpture (plate 131). In one a young man, in the other a young woman (plate 106), stood alongside stylized vegetation to symbolize the humanity that received the gift of fire. The architects didn't care for these side groups, so they were moved to a garden on the roof of the adjoining Palazzo d'Italia (plate 133).

Recently they have been returned to the plaza—not, however, to their intended ledges but to the level of the skating rink.

In 1933 Manship exhibited his recent work at Averell House, his first show of consequence in New York since 1916 and his last in a commercial gallery. He showed the plasters of some of his monumental work—*Abraham Lincoln*—the *Hoosier Youth,* the animals from the zoo gates, and an unfinished *Celestial Sphere;* bronzes of his European period, such as the two *Europas* (plates 95–100), the *Indian Hunter and His Dog, Diana* and *Actaeon* (plates 93, 94); a pair of bronze candelabra he had just made for his own dining room; and a selection of his recent portraits. Manship had also been asked to create the inaugural medal for Franklin D. Roosevelt, who had been elected in the fall of 1932. He was excited at renewing contact with Roosevelt, whom he had gotten to know during World War I, when Roosevelt was Assistant Secretary of the Navy. At that time Manship had designed medals for the Navy, and since Roosevelt didn't trust the aesthetic judgment of his boss, Josephus Daniels, he had Manship submit his designs when he knew that Daniels was safely out of town.

131 Prometheus Fountain *in*
1935, with Boy and Girl
as originally installed

Pages 134–35
132 **PROMETHEUS**
FOUNTAIN, *1934*
Gilded bronze, two and
one-half times life size
Rockefeller Center
Properties
© *Rockefeller Group, Inc.*

After finishing *Prometheus* in late spring 1933 and delivering it to the Roman Bronze Foundry in Corona, New York, for casting, Manship took his family to Europe. They stopped in Paris, then went on to Cordon in the French Alps for the month of August and spent September at their favorite beach resort Les Sablettes, near Toulon. The Manships had made plans to spend that winter in Rome, where Paul was to have a studio at the American Academy. He settled the younger children with Louise in an apartment on the via Condotti and returned to New York with Isabel to attend to business. Before going back to Rome for the winter the Manships attended a reception at the White House. The spring of 1934 saw the dedication of two of Manship's major works. *Prometheus* was unveiled at Rockefeller Center, and the Paul Rainey gates were dedicated at the Bronx Zoo. Paul and Isabel again left the children in Rome and returned to New York for these events.

These had been very productive years. The three major works, created simultaneously, are remarkable in many ways, but not least for their dissimilarity one is a heroic portrait statue of a national hero, imbued with the gravity due the subject; another is a nude mythological figure in flight, like one of Manship's parlor sculptures enlarged to a colossal scale; and the third is an architectural structure ornamented with plants and animals. What links them all is their style —the highly decorative style of this time when Manship's work came closest to Art Deco. This wasn't a matter of influence but rather of zeitgeist. In Paris in the 1920s a certain sense of style was in the air, the air that Manship breathed.

Sir Joseph Duveen was a benefactor of the Tate Gallery in London and a friend and admirer of Paul Manship. In 1935 he arranged for a major exhibition of Manship's sculptures at the Tate. This was a considerable honor: the only living foreign sculptor previously so celebrated had been Auguste Rodin. Manship showed his animals from the Bronx Zoo gates, many other pieces of the last decade, such as *Europa* and *Diana*, and a number of portraits.[26] Outside, in front of the museum, too large to be placed inside, was a bronze *Celestial Sphere*, on which Manship had been working since the late 1920s. He had first proposed the piece, unsuccessfully, to Thomas Cochran for Phillips Academy in Andover, Massachusetts, and had exhibited an unfinished version in plaster at Averell House in 1933. The idea had originated with a five-foot glass sphere etched with images of the constellations that Eric Gugler had bought in Germany. For his own amusement Manship had begun to model images of the constellations in high relief on the glass; eventually he had the whole thing cast in plaster. He

133 Boy *and* Girl *from*
Prometheus Fountain,
*as installed on the roof of
the Palazzo d'Italia
Rockefeller Center
Properties
© Rockefeller Group, Inc.*

mounted the sphere on a base consisting of the figure of a flying blindfolded woman, signifying the unknown. It was this sphere (plate 135) that was exhibited in London and eventually sold to the city of Philadelphia, where it now stands in front of the Franklin Institute in Logan Square. Manship also had a fifteen-inch reduction made (plate 134), which became a popular library piece.

The idea of a celestial sphere continued to haunt Manship, and he was determined to execute it on a monumental scale. As was his way, Manship sought out authorities in the field. He struck up close friendships with the astronomers Clyde Fisher of the American Museum of Natural History in New York and Harlow Shapley of Harvard University. He studied astronomy, made frequent

visits to New York's Hayden Planetarium, and went stargazing, often with his son, John, whom he taught to recognize the constellations. But his interest was an artist's, not a scientist's; what fascinated him was the mythology of the heavens—Perseus and Andromeda, Orion, and Pegasus eternally delineated by their stars.

At this time the officers of the Woodrow Wilson Foundation approached Manship regarding a proposed monument to Wilson at the Palace of the League of Nations, which was then under construction in Geneva. His first idea was to do a set of monumental bronze doors for the new building, but when that idea was rejected, he suggested a celestial sphere, enlarged to monumental scale (plate 138). The response was positive, and in May 1936 Manship signed a contract to create a sphere fourteen feet in diameter, for which he was to be paid about 130,000 gold francs—all the money they had available.

While the celestial sphere was in the making, the Manship studio was tremendously busy. The sculptors Carl Schmitz, Henry Kreis, Angelo Colombo, and Giuseppe Massari were the principal assistants; young Herbert Lewis Kammerer was working on the sphere's lettering with (for a short time) Nathaniel Pousette-Dart's son Richard; Hyman Filtzer was in the cellar, making the plaster molds. It was a very complex task: the stars up to the fourth magnitude all had to be

136 *Centaurs and Lupus from*
   Celestial Sphere, 1030
   Detail of plate 138

137 *Self-portrait from*
   Celestial Sphere, 1030
   Detail of plate 138

accurately located, and the diverse images and bands of lettering had to be melded into a pleasing rhythm and a unity of science and art. The plaster model was finished by 1938, and Manship turned it over to the Florentine bronze founder Bruno Bearzi, who finished casting it during the summer of 1939.

The Manships were spending less time in Europe during these years. Once they were settled into their house on Seventy-second Street, they began a sched-

138 **WOODROW WILSON**
   MEMORIAL—
   CELESTIAL SPHERE,
   1030
   Bronze, gilded
   constellations,
   silvered stars,
   diameter: 13 ft. 0 in.
   Palais des Nations,
   Geneva

they] should at least join openly and wholeheartedly this movement for the preservation of their liberties."[27] At this time Manship was also seeing a good deal of Rockwell Kent and Hugo Gellert, who were among the leaders of the politically radical artists.

Manship rarely entered competitions for commissions, and when he did he was rarely successful, but he was intrigued by a project to erect a double equestrian monument in Baltimore to commemorate the meeting of generals Robert E. Lee

139 **THE PARTING OF GENERAL LEE AND STONEWALL JACKSON ON THE EVE OF CHANCELLORSVILLE,** *1936*
Plaster, height: 27 in.

and "Stonewall" Jackson on the eve of the battle of Chancellorsville. Manship created a handsome model (plate 139) but lost the commission to Laura Gardin Fraser, whose husband, James Earle Fraser, had something of a lock on public monuments. The possibility of another equestrian monument came up in the late 1930s when the city of Saint Louis was planning to erect a statue of General John J. Pershing, a native son of Missouri. But after extensive correspondence between the promoters and Manship, nothing came of this either.

New York City had scheduled a world's fair for the summer of 1939, and it was to contain a profusion of art. Manship was given one of the choicest sites— on the main mall, just below the large structures called the Trylon and the Perisphere, which became the fair's logo. The fair's architects were his close friends William and Geoffrey Platt, the sons of Charles Adams Platt, who gave him a free hand. Manship decided to create a monumental sundial with four sculptural groups signifying the times of day, set in a large reflecting pool. He did the preliminary studies (plate 140) in New York and then in the summer of 1938 took them to Paris, where Louis Paulin, who had developed a remarkably accurate machine for enlargement, would assist him. The whole family, with the

140 *Paul Manship working on* Time and the Fates Sundial, *1938*

144

141 **TIME AND THE FATES
SUNDIAL**, *1030*
*Bronze, 100⅝ x 130 in.;
length of gnomon: 27 ft.
Brookgreen Gardens,
Murrells Inlet, South
Carolina*

142 **TIME AND THE FATES
SUNDIAL** *at the New
York World's Fair, 1030*

exception of Pauline, sailed on the *Ile de France,* where they met the sculptor John Storrs and his wife returning from their last visit to America. The two sculptors had conflicting ideals but nonetheless struck up a close friendship. Manship rented a studio at Montrouge, on the edge of Paris, and stayed there to finish his work while Isabel, who now had learned to drive, took the children by car to Rome, where Paul was to meet them. The family returned to New York late in September, just as the European leaders were preparing to meet at Munich for their ill-fated effort to stave off war.

The *Time and the Fates Sundial* (plates 141, 142) and the four *Moods of Time* (plates 143–46) were in many ways Manship's favorite works. They summed up his obsession with time. He believed that a major purpose of art, especially of art in the classical tradition, was to reconcile the passage of time with permanence. The monumental groups, which were executed in staff (a plaster of Paris compound) for the world's fair, have been lost; but the working models of various sizes were done in bronze after the war (plate 144), and they are among Manship's most ingenious, complex, and inventive works.

Once the world's fair sculptures were in place, along with a plaster version of his *Woodrow Wilson Memorial—Celestial Sphere,* Manship busied himself with writing articles on decorative sculpture and on the history of sculpture for the *Encyclopedia Britannica.*[28] He had long reflected on the nature of his art and its

148

history, and this task permitted him to order and deepen his thoughts. He believed that for sculpture to be effective it must reflect the deepest ideals of a society rather than simply the personal ideas of the artist. His dissatisfaction with sculpture in his later years was that he felt it didn't attempt to express anything meaningful to any but a small self-appointed elite.

The New York World's Fair had been envisioned as a preview of the world of the future, but it became instead a summation of the fragile but rich culture of the years between the two world wars. After the war everything would be different —more crass, more practical, and without the fantasy and poetry of that earlier era—the poetry of Orpheus, in one of Manship's favorite images, playing the lyre at the edge of hell.

145 **MOODS OF TIME:**
DAY, *1938*
Staff
Destroyed

146 **MOODS OF TIME:**
NIGHT, *1939–40*
Staff
Destroyed

9 · WORLD WAR II

Ironically, September 1, 1939, the day that war began in Europe, was also the day that Manship's great bronze *Woodrow Wilson Memorial—Celestial Sphere* (plate 138) was installed at the doomed League of Nations, on the shores of Lake Geneva. The symbol of Wilson's great experiment now stood like a whale stranded on the beach, but fortunately the new United Nations took over the building after the war as its European headquarters.

Since there was now no major work in progress, Paul dismantled the sizable workshop he had put together during the 1930s. While he had enjoyed the chance to do large sculptures, he disliked being the boss of a busy enterprise: the record keeping, the requirements imposed by the new Social Security Administration, all of this seemed to conspire to keep him from his own work. Again, as in 1921, he was happy to give up all this activity and go

back to a simpler way, pursuing his own inspiration. Manship did not entirely give up his assistants. There was always a studio man, who swept the floor and cleaned the tools and did minor repairs; this was Gigi D'Olivo's job until the end of the war, when he could no longer handle it and was replaced by Eddy Zakavec. In addition, Manship had at least one professional assistant; during these years this was Herbert Lewis Kammerer. If there was more work to be done he might employ a second assistant for a time, but he never reactivated the busy workshop of the 1930s, when he had had seven or eight people working in the studio.

Without the pressure of commissions, Manship was able to assume positions within various art organizations, which he had previously avoided. In 1939 he became president of the National Sculpture Society and so remained until 1942,

147 **DANCING FIGURE**,
late 1040s
Crayon on paper

148 **GARDEN OF EDEN—
SUNDIAL**, *1041*
Detail of plate 150

152

returning in 1945–46 as acting president while Cecil Howard was doing war service. Manship also served on the council of the National Academy of Design and was its vice president from 1942 to 1948. He was a member of the Federal Art Commission, the New York City Art Commission, and the Smithsonian Art Commission, which he served as chairman until his death.

Nineteen-forty was a bad year. The triumph of the Germans in Scandinavia and Western Europe, and particularly the sudden collapse of France, had a traumatic effect on Isabel, who took to her bed with a recurrence of the phlebitis that had plagued her previously. Her ill health and the increasing difficulty of finding servants convinced the Manships to move next door into the duplex apartment that had originally been planned for Riccardo Bertelli and his family. During the summer of 1940 the Manships stayed in New York, although they drove Sarah Jane to Lake Winnepesaukee, New Hampshire, to visit friends and took the occasion to visit Clara Fargo Thomas in Bar Harbor and Booth Tarkington in Kennebunkport. The trip ended with a few weeks in Cape Ann. Among the attractions of Cape Ann was the close proximity of Manship's sculptor friends George Demetrios and Walker Hancock, who had studios in Lanesville, as well as painters such as Gifford Beal, Harrison Cady, Anthony Thieme, and Max Kuehne in Rockport. Isabel and the children liked the area, finding it a welcome change from the increasingly suburban Fairfield County, so in subsequent years they were to rent a house in Pigeon Cove for the summer. Pauline became friendly there with a young man of Finnish extraction—Ilmari Natti, called Jimo. They were married on July 4, 1943. The Manships became related to the sculptor Walker Hancock through their marriage, as he was married to Jimo's sister. Chou Chou was not at the wedding, for she had volunteered to serve with the WAAC, and she was to be posted in New Guinea and the Philippines.

It was in 1940 that Mrs. James Longstreet appeared on the scene. Remarkably, seventy-five years after the end of the Civil War, the widow of one of the South's leading generals was still active. Her mission was to erect a monument at Gettysburg to her husband, one of the very few major southern warriors who had not been so honored. She wanted Manship to do the work, and he happily began a sketch for yet another equestrian statue, hoping that this time he would have the chance to complete it (plate 149). But he was foiled again. Mrs. Longstreet, for all her energy and devotion, could not raise the money. Perhaps the age of equestrian monuments was over. In any case, when the United States declared war in December 1941, the project was dropped, and the indefatigable Mrs. Longstreet spent the war years working as a riveter.

149 **SKETCH FOR LONGSTREET MEMORIAL**, *1940*
Plaster

150 **GARDEN OF EDEN—
SUNDIAL,** *1041*
*Bronze, height: 36½ in.;
diameter of sphere: 20½
in.; height of Adam: 13
in.; height of Eve: 11 in.;
diameter of base: 11 in.*

The only important work that Manship did at this time was the *Garden of Eden—Sundial* (plate 150), the last of his sundials intended for private gardens. It is a handsome piece, with a massive but compact composition in which the figures of Adam and Eve are intertwined with the Tree of Life. Manship seemed to be moving away from the linear and decorative style that had originally brought him fame. But with the United States at war, Manship's business quickly ground to a halt. The foundries were converted to war work, and bronze was unavailable. The only way a sculptor could have his work cast was to sacrifice an existing work. Manship clarified this in a letter to Jacques Lipchitz, who was hoping to find a way around the order: "[This] means that I may melt a piece of my bronze, but may not use scrap material from any other source. None of the sculptors, I believe, wish to interfere in any way with the production of war materials." In any event, there were almost no commissions for anything so frivolous as sculpture. The work that Manship did between 1942 and 1945 was almost all for his own pleasure and almost all in terra-cotta, since clay, at least, was not a vital war material.

During these years Manship turned once again to portraiture, now modeling the head in high relief in clay that would be fired, mounted on a wood panel, and framed. He had a number of his friends sit for him, including some of his colleagues from the National Academy of Arts and Letters, such as the writers Robert Frost, Booth Tarkington, and Van Wyck Brooks, as well as the painters Gifford Beal and Charles Hopkinson, the ornithologist Robert Cushman Murphy, War Secretary Henry L. Stimson, and others. There were a few portrait commissions, too—notably, one of the president of the Singer Sewing Machine Company, Sir Douglas Alexander, which was executed in marble (plate 151). Sir Douglas was so taken with his bust that he had a number of copies made, as well as a relief portrait done in terra-cotta in

151 **SIR DOUGLAS ALEXANDER**, *1944*
Marble, height: 18¾ in.;
base: 6¼ x 6¼ in.

various sizes, to be distributed among the company offices. The Alexander commission was a welcome sinecure during these lean years.

For lean they were. Paul had previously lived at the edge of his income, and the sudden reduction in income led to rather hard times. He had taken a loss of about ten thousand dollars on the *Woodrow Wilson Memorial—Celestial Sphere,* and now he was forced to sell the Lincoln Life Insurance Company stock that he had taken in partial payment for *Abraham Lincoln—the Hoosier Youth* (plate 115). He was to regret this after the war, when the stock appreciated enormously. In order to earn extra money, he began lecturing and doing demonstrations, primarily for museums and women's clubs. These were quite successful, and his agency

152 PLASTILENE FIGURE FOR "PORTAL OF FREEDOM," *1942*

was able to book a number of appearances for him across the country. When Walker Hancock asked Paul to take over his classes at the Pennsylvania Academy of the Fine Arts, he was happy to do so. For the duration of the war and a couple of years afterward Manship spent two days each week in Philadelphia while school was in session. It was a kind of return to his youth, as Hancock himself had taken over Charles Grafly's class years before.

Manship never much liked teaching, considering it largely a waste of time. He judged most of the students to be without any real talent or any real intention of pursuing a career in the arts. One young student of minimal ability particularly irked him. When Manship told him rather forcefully that he was wasting both their time, the young man broke down, admitting that his psychiatrist had told him to study art. Manship exploded, telling the poor fellow to advise his psychiatrist to do his own work and not to pass it off on someone else. Nonetheless, he did have a few students during these years who became professional sculptors of some distinction, including Evangelos Frudakis, Edward Hoffman, and Karen Worth.

The French architect Jacques Carlu spent the war years in New York, where he had fled with his Jewish wife, the painter Natacha Carlu. Since neither he nor Manship had much to do, they would meet in the studio to plan large public monuments decorated with sculpture. Carlu had the happy idea of a *Portal of Freedom* (plate 152), based on the American flag, with stripes holding a band of stars, to be built at Battery Park in lower Manhattan—a dream, of course, as no government in the pragmatic United States would spend money on something so purely symbolic. In 1943 Manship won a federal competition for the design of a Four Freedoms postage stamp. That year he also modeled a plaque to commemorate American-Soviet friendship, which was presented to the Russian ambassador Andrei Gromyko, who wrote Manship a polite letter of thanks. And he sketched a number of memorials, including a group of aviation memorials (plates 153–55), in anticipation of a postwar demand.

During the summer of 1943 Manship began looking at property on Cape Ann to buy. It was a good time to do so. The local granite quarries had closed, and the Rockport Granite Company was in bankruptcy; its only business was the liquidation of its real estate. Paul therefore had a wide choice and eventually paid twenty-six hundred dollars for fourteen acres of quarry land in Lanesville, across the street from the Nattis' farmhouse and a short walk from the village—a distinct advantage during the war, when no one had a car. The property contained two handsome quarries filled with water, delightful for swimming in the summer and for skating in the winter. He and Eric Gugler chose a site alongside the smaller quarry, looking toward the steeple of the village church. Gugler's plan called for a house and studio united by an extensive grape arbor. Because it was still wartime, there was difficulty in acquiring building

153 **SKETCH FOR "AVIATION MONUMENT,"** *1941*
Plaster, life size
Destroyed by the artist

154 *Paul Manship working on plastilene model of Aviation Memorial (now destroyed) in his New York studio, 1941*

155 **CONQUEST OF THE SKIES—STUDY FOR "AVIATION MEMORIAL,"** *1043*
Plaster
John and Margaret Manship

156 *Paul Manship's studio
and house in Lanesville,
Massachusetts*

materials. When an old house in Pigeon Cove was offered for sale for five hundred dollars on the condition that it be moved, Paul bought it and had his carpenter, William Niemi, take the house apart and rebuild it according to Gugler's plans. For the arbor he bought the derricks from the granite pier at Pigeon Cove and had them cut into column lengths, inspiring his friend the architect Walker Cain to write a poem on the "Derrick Order"—a triple pun on derrick, Doric, and Eric (as in Gugler).

It may seem odd that Manship embarked on this ambitious building program at a time when it was hard to find workmen and materials and when he had to borrow money. But the project was a much-needed outlet for his pent-up crea-tive energy. The family moved into the house in the spring of 1945. It was then that Manship was able to buy a splendid oxen barn dating from the 1840s to use as a studio. Eino Natti, Jimo's older brother, carefully took the barn apart and rebuilt it where Gugler's plan called for a studio. Work on the Lanesville property continued through the 1950s. Manship made it a showcase for his sculpture, designing a terrace for the world's fair groups, which he had cast in bronze as soon as that became possible again. (These were eventually sold to Sterling Forest Gardens and replaced by Manship's great group of bears, plate 168.) Manship's proclivity for selling his sculpture directly out of his garden led Barry Faulkner to remark that he was selling sculpture "on the hoof."[29] He later designed a gazebo of espaliered pear trees to house a statue—first *Eve* and then the lovely marble *Leda* (plate 179)—and a fountain crowned by his bronze *Maenad* (plate 157), and a figure called *Spring* for the herb garden.

It was on Cape Ann that the Manships celebrated the end of the war in August 1945. Everyone was looking toward the future, but the postwar world of art would be very different from that before the war.

157 **MAENAD**, 1053
*Bronze, height: 34 in.;
diameter of base: 10 in.
John and Margaret
Manship*

10 · THE POSTWAR YEARS

The story of how the art scene in New York changed during the Second World War has been frequently told. The city was host to many European refugee artists, and under their influence the modern movement took root as it hadn't earlier. But fashion changes more slowly in sculpture than in painting, and for Manship 1945 didn't seem so different from 1940. In fact, he was optimistic about his own role in the postwar world. He was at the top of his profession, with honors coming to him from all over the world: corresponding membership in the Academia Nacional de las Bellas Artes in Argentina in 1944 and in the Académie des Beaux-Arts in Paris in 1946, and membership in the oldest of the academies —l'Accademia di San Luca in Rome—in 1952. In the spring of 1945 he was awarded the gold medal for sculpture by the National Institute of Arts and Letters and given a retrospective exhibition in its handsome galleries. But there was a worm in the apple: few reviews of his show appeared.[30] In 1948 Manship was elected president of the American Academy of Arts and Letters, succeeding Walter Damrosch, and in 1950 he was elected president of the Century Club.

Manship encountered a serious problem at the National Institute of Arts and Letters on account of his old friend Hunt Diederich, whom he and Barry Faulkner had successfully proposed for election to the Institute some years earlier. Now Diederich procured some of the Institute's letterhead and concocted a letter denouncing the Jews and their role in American life, which he sent to the newspapers. There was nothing for Manship and Faulkner to do but propose his expulsion from the Institute. Hunt's life was falling apart: he had badly broken his leg, which never healed, and to deal with the pain he had become addicted to cocaine; his wife, Wanda, had been killed when their house burned down; and their youngest son, Harold, was killed in Korea. Hunt himself died in 1954. While remaining his friend, Paul was deeply saddened to see his talented old companion in art and mischief destroy himself.

158 **IMMORTALITY**, *1952*
Detail of plate 105

159 **HERCULES**, *1945*
Bronze, height: 30 in.;
base: 17 x 7¾ in.

Manship's finances improved as soon as the war was over. He had several commissions to execute, the first of which was a statue of Hercules for the Hercules Powder Company in Wilmington, Delaware. This mythical figure was just his kind of job, and the resulting thirty-inch statue (plate 159) is a genial example of his work. Then there was a tablet in honor of Franklin D. Roosevelt (plate 160) for a synagogue in Pennsylvania. In this case the results were below Manship's usual standards, as perhaps was a statue he did of President Albert A. Murphree for the University of Florida. In portrait sculpture Manship always had a problem resolving the individuality of the subject with his classical leaning toward universality and abstraction. In both these cases the results were rather dull. A happier work from this time is a flagpole base (plate 161) for the Alfred E. Smith public housing project in downtown Manhattan, near the Brooklyn Bridge. Robert Moses, New York City's powerful parks commissioner and the Pooh-Bah of New York's bureaucracy, asked Manship to recommend a sculptor for the job. Moses suggested portraying the animals that had run wild in Manhattan before the arrival of the Europeans, an idea that interested Manship enough to do it himself, even though little money was involved. He executed the

160 **FRANKLIN D. ROOSEVELT MEMORIAL**, *1945*
Bronze, 43 x 23½ x 6 in.
Reform Congregation
Keneseth Israel, Elkins
Park, Pennsylvania

161 **SKETCH FOR "ALFRED E. SMITH MEMORIAL FLAGPOLE BASE,"** *1940*
Plastilene

work quickly, by his technique of direct modeling in plaster, and sent it to the foundry. It consists of a drum with deer in high relief, above them a striding bear, and at the top an owl and a beaver.

There were other commissions as well, including several portraits: the boy Timmy Betts and his stepfather Joseph McMullan, Dr. Satterwhite of Louisville, Kentucky, and posthumous ones of his cousin Charles Manship and his friend John Senior (made from a death mask). There were also a number of medals: to honor the Antarctic expeditions, the Welfare Council of New York City, the World Government Association, the Audubon Society, and the American Historical Preservation Society. Manship also did a twenty-inch silver plaque of the

Missouri state seal (plate 162) for the battleship *Missouri*; a plaque for Federal Hall honoring George McAneny; and a heroic-size portrait of Alexander Graham Bell for Bell Laboratories in Murray Hill, New Jersey. But of all the commissions that crowded in on him during these postwar years—and it seems that in his eagerness to improve his finances he turned nothing down— the most successful was a nude figure for the garden of Houghton Metcalf in Middleburg, Virginia. *Susanna* (plate 163), a kneeling girl rubbing herself with a cloth that is wrapped around one leg, shows Manship at his most classical and lyrical.

During the Red scare of the late 1940s and early '50s Manship was named by Representative George A. Dondero, of the House Un-American Activities Committee, as one of the communist-leaning artists of the 1930s. Dondero's diatribe, on March 25, 1949, was as far as the matter went; Paul was not asked to testify. He had unquestionably been supportive of left-wing causes, having been active in the formation of the American Artists Congress and having taken a public stand on the Spanish Civil War; but by the time of World War II his political views had changed radically. His eyes had been opened by the revelations concerning the Moscow purge trials and the massacres done on Stalin's order, with the Hitler-Stalin pact of 1939 as the last straw. By the 1950s he had veered to the opposite side, regularly voting Republican and greatly admiring General Dwight D. Eisenhower.

162 **SEAL OF THE STATE OF MISSOURI**, *1940*
Silver, diameter: 21 in.
U.S.S. Missouri

163 **SUSANNA**, *1048*
Marble, height: 37 in.; base: 10 x 15 in.

Manship's left-wing past was the basis for a campaign against him by his erstwhile friend the sculptor Wheeler Williams. Williams publicly accused Manship of being a communist, especially before the boards of various organizations in which they were both active—the Century Club, the National Academy of Design, and the National Sculpture Society. But his charges were so grotesque as to seem ludicrous, and they were ultimately more damaging to Williams than to Manship, who endured the barbs with a certain equanimity. Once in Florence in the Piazza della Signoria, while looking at Baccio Bandinelli's *Hercules and Cacus,* he said to his son, John, "Wheeler Williams is the Bandinelli of our time." The reference is not only to Bandinelli's relative incompetence but also to his notorious hatred and envy of Michelangelo.[31]

When it was possible to travel again after the war, Manship went to Italy to check on the condition of the American Academy and of the bronze foundries. He found that his friend Bruno Bearzi had reopened his foundry, which had been bombed during the attack on Florence, and was now ready to do business. From then on, Manship had Bearzi cast almost all of his pieces, unless a tight schedule required the use of a New York foundry or the work was too large for Bearzi to handle. Manship also had his marble work done in Florence by a shop near the Porta Romana. During the war he had had this work done by Edmondo Quattrocchi in New York. Although he had not been trained as a marble carver, Manship always worked extensively over the surface of pieces when they came back from the shops, sharpening the details until they satisfied him. Manship and his family spent the summer of 1950 in Rome, where the Academy put an apartment and studio at his disposal. While there, Sarah Jane fell in love with a classmate of John's from Harvard, Edwin Murtha, and they were married in New York the following year.

Manship now established a routine that he would follow for the rest of his life. At some time during the year he would make a trip to Europe, going to Florence to work at the foundry, to Rome to stop in at the Academy, and often to Paris to visit his old friend Welles Bosworth. During the warm seasons he would travel back and forth to Lanesville, Massachusetts, but unfortunately his asthma made it impossible for him to stay there long, and after two or three weeks he would have to hurry back to New York to recover in its impure but pollenless air. The rest of the time he spent working in his New York studio. He rarely used his great studio in Lanesville, except for small pieces. One exception was the statue of John Hancock (plate 164), commissioned by the John Hancock Life Insurance Company to adorn their building near Copley Square in Boston. Monumental

164 *Bruno Bearzi and Paul Manship with the plaster of* John Hancock *in Bearzi's workshop in the Uffizi Gallery, Florence, August 4, 1949*

165 **IMMORTALITY**, *1952*
Marble high relief,
heroic size
American Military
Cemetery, Nettuno, Italy

portrait statues of national heroes had been the principal work of the masters of Manship's youth—John Quincy Adams Ward, Augustus Saint-Gaudens, and Daniel Chester French—and he was always interested in trying his hand at the genre, although his genius lay in other directions. The Hancock figure was, on the whole, a success. Interestingly, the company acquired the plaster model as well as the finished bronze to insure that the bronze would be unique; then, in one of those strange acts of corporate housecleaning, a few years ago they sold the plaster.

Eric Gugler had been awarded the commission to design the American military cemetery in Nettuno, Italy. It was there that the men who had died in the campaigns in southern Italy were buried, including those who had fallen at the bloody landing at Anzio and Nettuno. Gugler naturally wanted Manship to do the sculpture for the memorial, and together they went to Italy to study the site, a field on a gentle slope. Gugler planned to place the memorial building at the top of the hill, where an ancient stone pine was growing. His plan called for an open court containing the tree, flanked by a chapel on the left and a museum of the southern Italian campaign on the right. In the center of the court Manship placed a bronze group of two servicemen walking arm in arm (plate 166). On the façades of these side buildings he created two heroic marble reliefs entitled *Memory* and *Immortality* (plate 165), which portray two draped female figures, one laying a wreath on the men's graves, the other carrying a dead soldier heavenward. The predominant emotion is elegiac, an old man's meditation on the loss of youth. Paul had not experienced this loss in his own family, but he did have friends who had lost their sons.

166 **COMRADES IN ARMS**,
1953
Bronze, heroic size
American Military
Cemetery, Nettuno, Italy

In December 1951 the Metropolitan Museum held a large exhibition of American sculpture. To satisfy all factions they had two juries, abstract and figurative, and Manship served on the figurative one. As his own exhibit in the show he sent the plaster model of the Anzio-Nettuno servicemen, and for the first time in his life he was clobbered by the critics. Emily Genauer in the *Herald Tribune* and Howard Devree in the *Times* both compared the work to department-store dummies. The fact that the work was in white plaster certainly didn't help—it does look better in bronze—but the classicizing abstraction has been carried so far that the piece does seem vapid and expressionless, the young men without character. The decision to render them half-naked and without marked personal characteristics may also have been a mistake. They were meant to stand for all the American youths who had gone to fight in Europe, but here all is perilously close to nothing.

If this work was a comparative failure, Manship's next important one was a complete success. Friends of William Church Osborn, who had been president of the Metropolitan Museum of Art, had raised money for a monument to him in Central Park near the museum, and Robert Moses, the parks commissioner, suggested that Manship would be the right man for the job. It was decided to make a pair of bronze gates for the children's playground (plate 167). Manship chose as his subject scenes from *Aesop's Fables:* the crane and the peacock, the wolf and the lamb, and the country mouse and the city mouse were on one side; on the other were the fox and the crow, and the hare and the tortoise. The frame is crowned with squirrels, and the gates are set between two granite piers, on which were placed small groups of bears and deer from the models done for the gates for the Bronx Zoo (plate 169). The Osborn gates are in high relief, modeled on both sides, with a pierced background. Highly decorative, they have great charm and humor. When the museum was expanded in the early 1970s, the gates were moved uptown along with the playground, but unfortunately the protective grilles were not included in the reconstruction, and in the mid-1970s the work was seriously vandalized: one of the gates was demolished, although most of the pieces were found, and the group of deer was pried loose and stolen. At this

167 **DRAWING FOR OSBORN MEMORIAL GATES**, *1951*
Pencil on paper, 9 x 11 in.

168 **GROUP OF BEARS**,
1932 (cast in 1984)
Bronze, 88 x 30 x 56 in.
The Metropolitan Museum of Art, New York; Gift of Sheila W. and Richard T. Schwartz in honor of Lewis I. Sharp, 1989

Pages 170–77
169 **GATEWAY TO THE WILLIAM CHURCH OSBORN MEMORIAL PLAYGROUND**, *1952*
Bronze, 95 x 100 in.
Central Park, New York

writing the gates are in storage, pending restoration.

Having done *Aesop's Fables* for the gates, Manship was considered the right man for a sculpture inspired by *Alice in Wonderland*. He refused, on the grounds that there wasn't enough money involved to justify the time and effort involved. José De Creeft did the work; it is his best-known and most beloved sculpture but certainly his most uncharacteristic. When the Osborn gates were finished, Manship held an open house in his studio to show them to his friends. Given the recent attack by critics, he had no desire to risk a public showing. In the summer of 1953 he took the work to Florence to have it cast by Bearzi.

The gates were the last important work to be done in the Seventy-second Street studio. The property was becoming a real burden. Paul had bought it at the height of the market in 1925, but during the Depression he had had to lower the rents. When the war came the rent-control

THE CRANE ALOFT SURVEYS THE WORLD · · THE EARTHBOUND PEACOCK STRUTS AND BOASTS ·

THE CITY MOUSE AND THE COUNTRY MOUSE

Woe to the Lamb that disputes the Wolf

regulations indefinitely fixed the low Depression rates. Worse yet, the city codes were getting increasingly severe, and many features of the buildings that had previously been legal had now become violations. The final straw was a fire in the stairwell of number 321, for which Paul was sued. There were too many aggravations, and he was eager to retire from being a landlord.

He sold the property in 1954, with one of the conditions of the sale that the Manships move out, as the new owners intended to tear down the five old buildings and replace them with a large apartment house. Manship rented a studio in an old townhouse at 10 East Seventeenth Street and an apartment for Isabel and himself at 21 Gramercy Park. He moved without regret. All his life he had forged ahead without looking back, and although he had invested a good deal of himself, of his talent and dreams in the house and studio on Seventy-second Street, he was quite willing to sacrifice all of this for the freedom to pursue his art.

11 · A CREATIVE OLD AGE

Nineteen fifty-four was a year of renunciations and beginnings. Paul sold his property and resigned as president of the Academy of Arts and Letters and of the Century Club. All his life he had been acutely aware of the passage of time, and now, facing his seventieth birthday, he was shedding all unnecessary encumbrances to be ready for a productive old age. He was in remarkably good health for a man facing seventy, but age inevitably took its toll. He broke his leg in Lanesville in 1955 by falling from a ladder while pruning his grapes. It took a while to recover, and during the summer he went to take the cure at Abano Terme, in Italy, with Eric Gugler. Paul suffered disequilibrium caused by inner-ear problems as well as chronic asthma, which in the end would affect his heart.

He lived a very regular life, devoting most of his time to work. When he finished at the studio for the day, he'd go to the National Arts Club at Gramercy Park, have a drink or two with friends, and then to bed early after a light supper. He would get up around eight, fix his breakfast, and walk to the studio, where he would spend an hour on his correspondence and business and then get to work on sculpture. Eddy Zakavec, the studio man, prepared lunch (the day's principal meal) for Paul, himself, the assistant, and an occasional guest. Then they went back to work until after five. This regularity gave Manship the freedom to create a large body of work in the decade before his death.

The studio he rented was in a formerly attractive townhouse in the once-fashionable area of Union Square. Bertie Gallatin, Manship's old friend, said that as a boy he had visited an elderly relative who lived in that very house, but it had since fallen on hard times. Manship had the first floor—a long, rather narrow space without windows, lit by fluorescent tubes. The first important work to be executed there was another commission that came his way through Robert Moses. Among his many hats, Moses wore that of chairman of the Triborough Bridge and Tunnel Authority, which was sponsoring the construction of the New

170 **LEDA**, *1961*
Detail of plate 170

York Coliseum, a large exhibition and convention center on Columbus Circle. The architecture of the building was functional and plain, and Moses asked Manship what could be done to make the exterior more interesting. Moses, Manship, and the architects—the Levi brothers—decided to ornament it with four large seals of the governmental bodies involved: the United States of America, the State of New York, the City of New York, and the Triborough Bridge and Tunnel Authority (plate 171). These were to be twelve feet square and cast in aluminum. Moses was so pleased with Manship's work for the Coliseum that he asked him to work on another project, this one for the Saint Lawrence

171 **SEAL OF THE TRIBOROUGH BRIDGE AND TUNNEL AUTHORITY**, *1055*
Aluminum, 120 x 120 in.

172 **SEAL OF THE POWER AUTHORITY OF THE STATE OF NEW YORK**, *1050*
Plaster, diameter: 20 in.

Seaway, of which Moses was also chairman. For the Power Authority building at Massena, New York, Manship modeled the seals of the United States and the State of New York, and created one for the New York State Power Authority (plate 172). For the dam across the Saint Lawrence River he made the seals of the United States and Canada in gilded bronze set against a black marble background.

Robert Moses was known as a decisive leader who brooked no opposition. In Manship's first encounter with him they had been on opposite sides of an issue —the plan for a Battery-to-Brooklyn Bridge. It was out of character for Moses to forgive an opponent, but in this case he did; he learned to trust Manship and was happy with his work. At least two exceptionally fine works of sculpture resulted from their collaboration: the two sets of gates made for Central Park. First were the Osborn gates, for which Moses had recommended Manship. Then, in the late 1950s, Moses suggested that a monumental gate (plate 173) by Manship might be appropriate for the children's zoo that Governor Herbert Lehman was

173 **HERBERT LEHMAN GATEWAY FOR THE CHILDREN'S ZOO**, *1061*
Bronze and granite,
18 x 20½ ft.
Children's Zoo, Central Park, New York

174 **BOY WITH GOATS**
(detail of Herbert
Lehman Gateway), *1000*
Plaster
The boy was posed by the
artist's grandson,
Erik Natti.

donating to Central Park, to be near the old zoo and close to the apartment house where the Lehmans lived.

For the gate's lintel Manship modeled a floral swath filled with birds, on which he set a group of a boy dancing between two goats (plate 174). The subject recalls his *Dancer and Gazelles* (plate 65) of 1916, but the differences are as important as the similarities. Here is a boy doing a vigorous peasant dance with goats rather than a girl performing a sensuous Oriental dance with deer; robust and realistic forms have replaced the linear design of the earlier work. The gate, dedicated in 1961, is a remarkable expression of joy, an affirmation of life and youth by a man then seventy-five years old.

Very soon after moving downtown, Paul and Isabel had to leave the apartment on Gramercy Park. The building was a cooperative, and the board offered them a choice of buying the apartment or moving out. Having just escaped from being a landlord, Manship had no intention of ever again owning real estate in New York, even a share in an apartment house. They found a small apartment in the National Arts Club, essentially one room with a kitchenette and bath, and moved there in 1956. This was to be their home until Manship's death there ten years later. In 1958 the old house where Manship had his studio succumbed to many years of neglect and abuse and was torn down to make way for a parking lot. So Manship moved his studio again, this time to a floor in a fine old cast-iron building at Twentieth Street and Broadway, built in the 1860s to house Lord and Taylor's department store. This handsome, spacious, and thoroughly satisfactory studio served the sculptor until his death.

The small apartment in the National Arts Club was satisfactory to Paul, who used it only at night for sleeping, but Isabel was living there all alone during the day. Lonely and depressed, she tended to drink too much. Since the 1930s she had tended to seek consolation in alcohol, but it was only now that this became serious. Her physician told Manship that some solution would have to be found for the underlying problem, which was loneliness, or she might have to go into an institution. The solution was for her to live in Rome with her daughter and son-in-law, Sarah Jane and Edwin Murtha. The results were satisfactory for everyone, and in order to be with Isabel, Manship increased the time he spent in Italy each year. During the summers Sarah Jane and her daughter Anne accompanied Isabel back to Lanesville.

Manship wanted a book published on his work. The only one of consequence so far had been Paul Vitry's, published in French almost thirty years earlier, and Manship realized that a generation was growing up not knowing who he was. No publisher wanted to risk doing a book on an artist who was increasingly out of fashion, but Macmillan was willing to distribute a book paid for by Manship. He employed his son-in-law Edwin Murtha to do the text. Murtha had the sense to realize that his greatest service would be to put together as good a catalog as possible, rather than a belletristic effusion, and the resulting book, published in 1957, has proven invaluable over the years to dealers, auctioneers, and scholars.

Meanwhile, Paul was spending a good deal of time with Eric Gugler. The men often lunched together at the Century Club or played pool there in the evenings and when Paul was alone in New York, he would often go to the Guglers' house in Snedens Landing for the weekend. It was natural for Paul to become involved in Gugler's projects. These included a dream project for a hall of history—a colossal stone hall, on the scale of the Temple of Karnak, with scenes from American history carved in granite on the walls and inscriptions explaining the events. Manship helped with the sculpture. There were flurries of interest in the project, but nothing ever happened, and the plans and models were destroyed in a fire that consumed Gugler's studio at Snedens Landing after his death.

A more successful and profitable venture was a memorial to Theodore Roosevelt (plate 175). Shortly after Roosevelt's death in 1919 a group of his friends and admirers purchased an island in the Potomac River, which was set aside as a wildlife sanctuary in his memory. By the 1950s it had been decided to place a national memorial to Roosevelt on the island, and Eric Gugler received the commission to design it. His plan was to open a formal plaza at one end of the island, which would otherwise be left in its natural state. In the center of this plaza he planned to place a great armillary sphere, but this plan went awry when Alice Longworth, Roosevelt's daughter, was shown a sketch of the sphere and said it looked like a child's jungle gym. It was then resolved to place a heroic-size portrait statue of Roosevelt in the spot, and so Manship embarked on his last major work.

The pose, Roosevelt standing with his arm raised, was chosen by his family. It was a characteristic gesture, taken from a photograph made while he was campaigning. Following his usual practice, Manship modeled a small study, which—after it was accepted—he enlarged to a figure twenty-four inches high. From this he created the finished model, a statue nine feet tall, working during the entire winter of 1962–63. He had a tailor in Rome make a Prince Albert coat, and when John returned to New York in January he was drafted to wear it and pose as Roosevelt. Paul used Roosevelt's death mask for the portrait head. When the model was finished to Manship's satisfaction he shipped it to Paris, where it was enlarged. Manship had to work very little on the final model. His hundred-thousand-dollar contract with the Department of the Interior was for only the model in plaster, although he advised on the choice of a foundry and was paid to supervise the casting.

The armillary sphere that was originally conceived for the Roosevelt memorial was recycled as a permanent sculpture for the New York World's Fair of 1964–65 (plate 176). It included the last and finest set of Manship's zodiac signs and a central group of an old man and a boy (plate 177). This group symbolized the continuity of time, with the old man transmitting his wisdom and ideals to the youth. The sphere remained in Flushing Meadow Park after the fair was over,

175 *Paul Manship with the newly cast* Theodore Roosevelt Memorial *in the Battaglia Foundry, Milan, December 1905*

184

but unfortunately it proved to be less than permanent. At some point in the mid-1970s it was destroyed and carted away, presumably to be sold as scrap metal.

With the Theodore Roosevelt memorial well under way, Eric Gugler was asked to design a memorial in Washington, D.C., for another Roosevelt, Franklin. The architect Marcel Breuer had been selected in a competition to design the memorial, but Congress hadn't liked his plan and refused to vote the money to build it. Gugler was brought in at the request of the Roosevelt family, and he intended to place a portrait statue of FDR in the middle of a formal garden. He asked Manship to do a sketch for the statue, but that was as far as the matter got; no monument has been built—an object lesson regarding what can happen when contradictory forces in the art world are of equal strength. When John F. Kennedy was elected president in 1960, Manship modeled the inaugural medal; Kennedy sat for him that December in William Walton's house in Georgetown.

Manship did commissioned work during these late years to pay his bills, but he also worked on a number of pieces for his own pleasure. He was not exhibiting and rarely sold works to collectors, so these pieces were really done for himself,

176 *Paul Manship's* Armillary Sphere *at the New York World's Fair of 1964–65, in front of the* Unisphere

177 **OLD MAN AND BOY —MODEL FOR ARMILLARY SPHERE,** *1963* Plastilene

They included the wonderful *Maenad* (plate 157) for his garden in Lanesville, a figure designed completely in three dimensions that shows the distance he had traveled from the decorative, rather two-dimensional works of his youth; and the *Leda* (plate 179), a marble work representing the final resolution of a theme with which he had wrestled since the 1920s. The subject is a nude woman with her hands in her hair and two putti at her feet. Manship had worked earlier on this idea to the extent of creating a life-size group in plaster (plate 178), which he later destroyed. The new *Leda* was delivered to Lanesville and set up in the pear-tree gazebo. He had originally entitled the work *Cassandra* but thought the title inappropriate and asked John what it should be called. John suggested *Leda*, who was the mother of the twin boys Castor and Pollux. The title didn't matter much anyway; what mattered was the rhythm of this most classical of Manship's nudes.

The main work of Manship's old age was a series of small bronzes modeled originally in wax and cast as unique pieces by the lost-wax process (plates 181–83, 187, 188). He had begun doing these works, which he called his "pet creations," in the 1930s, modeling figures in wax the way someone else might knit or do crossword puzzles. He carried a cigar box of wax and toothpicks to use as armatures, especially on his frequent transatlantic flights. He experimented with all types of subjects, often using a semiprecious stone as a base, and the work was done with the freedom and assurance that result from half a century of experience. These pieces are like lyric poems and are probably Manship's most deeply personal works; he was very reluctant to sell any of them. The series was almost intact when he died and was divided between the two museums that were his principal beneficiaries.

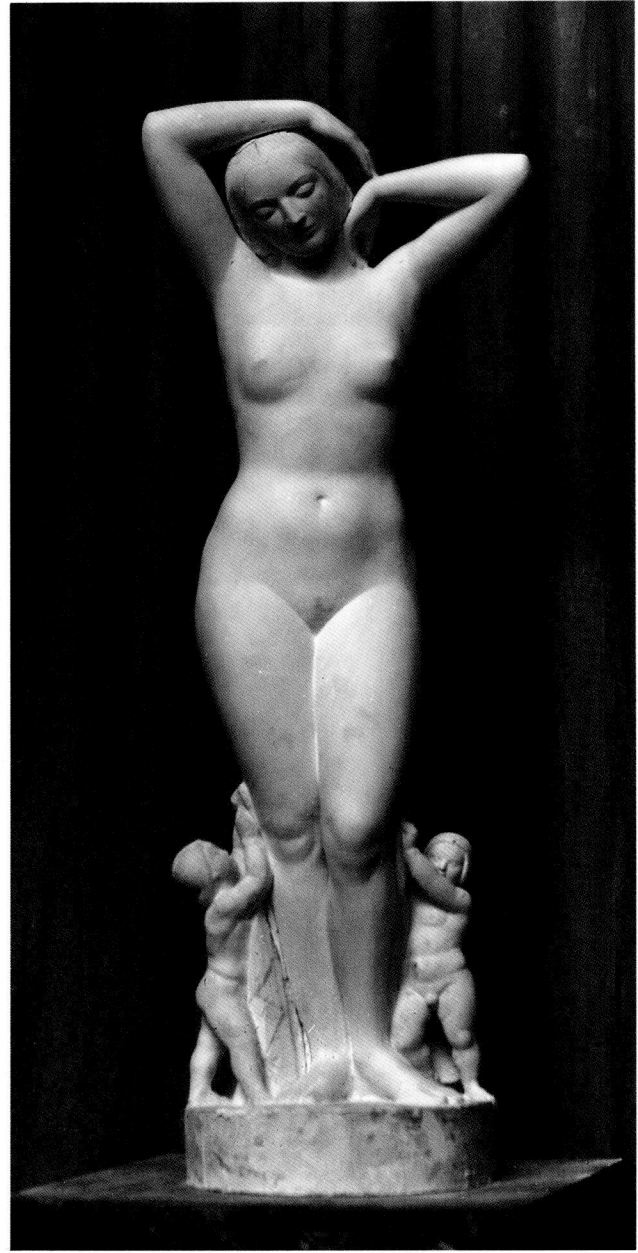

178 **LEDA**, *1920s*
Plaster
Destroyed by the artist

179 **LEDA**, *1901*
Marble, nearly life size
Installed in Paul
Manship's garden,
Lanesville,
Massachusetts

Paul was not only flying to Europe, he was also traveling frequently to California and Minnesota. He had always felt responsible for his family, but now the ease of air travel made it possible to see more of them. When he went to Saint Paul to model portraits of the founders of the 3-M Company, he got to know his nephews and nieces. And in California he went to see his sister Mary in Manhattan Beach and mourned her when she died in 1961. In California, too, he'd visit Chou Chou and her family in San Francisco and his sculptor friends Albert Stewart and Donal Hord.

On his frequent trips to Italy, Paul renewed his friendship with Bernard Berenson. When he presented Berenson with a copy of Murtha's book on his sculpture, BB said he was especially impressed with Manship's drawings and agreed to write a foreword for a book on them. As he was then well into his nineties, this project never materialized. One sorrow of growing old is losing one's friends and contemporaries. Manship expressed some of his feelings about death and survival in the funeral oration he delivered for his friend the cellist Willem Willeke in 1951: "Death," he said, "is not extinguishing the light . . . it is putting out the lamp because the dawn has come." Manship's religion was that of a pious pagan, like Socrates or Marcus Aurelius. He believed that the universe is orderly and harmonious and that the artist's job is to portray this harmony; art, he felt (citing Berenson), should be life-enhancing, never dwelling on death. He also believed in an eternal stability underlying the restless movement of time.

Manship was dissatisfied with the general direction of the art world during the 1950s and '60s, and he was especially unhappy with developments at the American Academy in Rome. He was its first great alumnus and had remained close to the Academy throughout the years, long serving as one of its trustees. After the war, when Laurance Roberts became director, things began to change: the artists selected for fellowships often had little or no interest in the classical art that had justified placing the Academy in Rome. Roberts invited some major modern artists to stay at the Academy, men like Henry Moore and Marino Marini. Although Manship did not see eye-to-eye with them, he could understand their work because they conceived of sculpture somewhat as he did. The real break came in the 1960s, when the Academy welcomed sculptors of the welding and assembling schools. Manship looked on these people as barbarians who should be kept out of the civilized city.

In 1961 he and Sidney Waugh were the sculptor members of the Fine Arts Committee of the Academy in Rome. They nominated the members of the jury for the following year but saw their nominations overturned by the committee, which was dominated by nonsculptors who instead named Isamu Noguchi, Theodore Roszak, and Jack Zajac. Manship was furious and wrote a long, blistering letter to the executive committee of the Academy. He was fighting a rearguard action in a losing battle and knew it, but he wanted to defend his ideal of art, even if he was to be labeled an old fogy, or worse. "I was in Florence recently," he wrote, "and talked to a young American sculptor, who when I asked him if he did not admire the Masterpieces of Florentine Art said, 'Yes, but those works have nothing to do with today.' So in not feeling the universality of great art he revealed his befogged state of mind and his own enclosed consciousness. He competes, as do we all within our understanding and competence, with the images to which we aspire, to him the great works of the past are road blocks to progress rather than wonderful stimulants to an expansive vision; and meaningful emulation is the reason to send men to study in Italy. Why send men there who could just as well carry out their work in Hoboken or San Diego?"

On the first of January 1963, Paul and Isabel celebrated their golden wedding anniversary with a splendid dinner party in the Twentieth Street studio, followed the next day with a reception. The family had gathered from around the world: Pauline with her husband and children were already in New York; Chou Chou and her family came from California; Sarah Jane and hers came from Rome, as did John and his fiancée, the sculptor Margaret Cassidy. Paul made a substantial gift to Grace Church to commemorate the wedding fifty years earlier.

182 **PEGASUS**, *1936*
Bronze and crystal,
height: 7 in.

12 · THE END AND A NEW BEGINNING

Manship was now traveling to Italy two or three times a year. His family was there and much of his work was there too, at Bearzi's foundry in Florence. By 1964 he was entering his eightieth year, and although he scarcely had a morbid concern with death, he could not help but be aware that his own might be coming soon. He therefore resolved to devote the next year to getting his affairs in order.

In March 1964 the U.S. Department of the Interior accepted the sculptor's recommendation that his statue of Theodore Roosevelt—which he had had enlarged in Paris—be cast by the Battaglia Brothers Foundry in Milan. They were set up to handle large work and had bid a very low price to do it. He traveled from New York to Europe to arrange the transport of the plaster from Paris to Milan. With this out of the way, he went back to New York to pursue his dream for a final major work—two groups of pioneers (plates 185, 186) for the steps of the Capitol in Washington. He had been speaking to the responsible people—the Architect of the Capitol and others—and found them interested, but no one was willing to make a commitment. So Manship proceeded on his own. He wanted to see two sculptural groups placed on the site of the nineteenth-century marble groups that had been removed during the renovation of the East Front. The new groups were to be based on the primary events of our history, the founding of the colonies in the seventeenth century and the push westward during the nineteenth. During the spring of 1965 he modeled his *Settlers of the West* at about one-eighth of final

183 **PEGASUS**, *1937*
Bronze on marble base,
8 x 2¹⁵/₁₆ x 2½ in.
National Museum of
American Art,
Smithsonian Institution,
Washington, D.C.;
Gift of the Estate of
Paul Manship

184 **EURYDICE**, *1935*
Detail of plate 188

scale; that is, with figures about one foot tall. He did not get to the other group until the end of the year.

During the summer of 1965 he had Eino Natti and Eddy Zakavec take all the plaster models out of the cupboards in Lanesville so that he could select the ones he wanted to save. Those he didn't were smashed behind the studio. Manship realized that his work was no longer as popular as it had once been and that a large number of sculptures left to his estate might burden rather than enrich it. The taxes levied on the art might wipe out the cash he left so that there wouldn't be enough to support Isabel in the style in which he wanted her to live. This was certainly a major reason for the provision in his will leaving almost all the work in his two studios to museums. But he had another motive: he wanted to leave a monument to himself. He had been impressed by the Musée Ingres in Montaubon, France; the Canova Museum in Possagno, Italy, which he had visited with John a few years earlier; and closer to home, the Saint-Gaudens Memorial in Cornish, New Hampshire, of which he was a trustee. There was also Chesterwood in Stockbridge, Massachusetts, which his friend Margaret Cresson was preparing as a museum to honor her father, Daniel Chester French.

For years Manship had been involved with the National Collection of Fine Arts (part of the Smithsonian Institution in Washington, D.C.; now called the National Museum of American Art). Until his death he served as chairman of the Smithsonian Art Commission, and he had been one of those responsible for procuring the old Patent Office Building as a home for the collection. It was therefore natural for him to name the museum as one of the principal beneficiaries of his will. As he expressed to David Scott, director of the collection, what he wanted was to have his work exhibited in a separate gallery. Scott responded sympathetically and suggested that Manship state his wishes in a letter, which the museum staff would then develop into a formal document. Manship wrote the letter[32] but the museum was in no hurry to proceed, and he died before anything was signed. The Smithsonian thus considered itself unfettered.

In September 1964 Laureen Tibbetts, who was then director of education for the Saint Paul Art Center (now called the Minnesota Museum of Art), called Paul in Lanesville and asked if she could visit him. She came with a letter from his childhood friend Ben Storey and convinced Manship of the importance of the museum that Saint Paul was organizing. When he got back to New York he rewrote his will, dividing his art between the National Collection of Fine Arts and the Saint Paul Art Center. It is likely that he expected his hometown to provide the memorial he wanted. These matters settled, he flew to Rome to celebrate Christmas and his eightieth birthday with Isabel and the Murthas. After Christmas he went to Milan to check on *Theodore Roosevelt* (plate 175), which was now in bronze. In the Murthas' Rome apartment, he finished the plastilene model for the *Settlers of the East* and gave it to Antonio Muzi to cast in plaster.

In his travels Manship had come down with a bad cold, which was aggravated by his chronic bronchial trouble. Back in New York in January he couldn't seem to shake it. The night of January 27 there was a formal dinner at the National Arts Club. Paul attended, but as he was feeling poorly he left early. He was expecting company for lunch at the studio the next day, and Eddy Zakavec got the meal ready, but when the guests arrived he had to tell them that Mr. Manship hadn't come in that day. This was on Friday, and by Monday, Eric Gugler, who had been calling frantically during the weekend, was convinced that something was seriously wrong. He went down to the National Arts Club and had the doorman open Paul's apartment. There they found him dead from a massive heart attack that had occurred while he was preparing breakfast Friday morning.

Pauline, who was in New York, arranged to have her father's body cremated, as he had requested. A memorial service was to be held later, at an unspecified date. John and Margaret came down from Boston as soon as they got the news, and as his father's executor John was responsible for the service. Though acknowledging that Paul had not been a church member, he thought it would please his mother to hold the service in Grace Church, where she had been married fifty-three years earlier. The church was crowded for the funeral on February 8. Dr. Robert Cushman Murphy, the well-known ornithologist and a close friend, read the eulogy, in which he incorporated some remarks by Barry Faulkner, who was then living in Keene, New Hampshire. That summer Paul's ashes were interred in his plot in Seaside Cemetery in Lanesville. Eddy Zakavec died in the fall of 1966; he had very little heart for living, as serving Manship had been his whole life. Isabel lived out her life quietly in Lanesville, dying in February 1974 in her ninety-first year.

Betti Richard, who had been a student of Manship's and was chairwoman of the art committee at the National Arts Club, put on a memorial exhibition at the club in April 1966. Margaret French Cresson held another memorial exhibition, at Chesterwood, during the summer of 1966. By that fall, almost all of Manship's work had been distributed to the two museums receiving his bequest. Within a month of Manship's death, the plaster of *Settlers of the East* was delivered to his studio. J. George Stewart, the Architect of the Capitol, was still very much interested and requested copies of the two groups. John had Cesare Contini make piece molds of the originals and two copies of each group. One of each was sent to Washington, D.C., where they were put on display in the basement gallery under the central Rotunda of the Capitol. But with time, and without Manship's presence, interest in the project diminished and died.

The monument to Theodore Roosevelt was inaugurated with great pomp on October 27, 1967. The principal speaker was Chief Justice Earl Warren; also present were the architect Eric Gugler; members of the Roosevelt family, notably Alice Longworth; the Secretary of the Interior, Stewart Udall, who was host on the occasion; and President Lyndon Johnson, who spoke and unveiled the gigantic statue. During the entire proceedings the name of Paul Manship was never mentioned. This proved a portent.

The *Washington Post* did mention Manship's name the following day, and again when the National Collection of Fine Arts held a memorial show in 1971, but then it was in order to launch a diatribe on Manship and the much-maligned Rayburn House Office Building. Manship had had nothing to do with that structure, other than making a marble portrait of Rayburn for it, but he was a convenient target for those who loathed its traditional classicism. The *Post*'s critic took the occasion to bury Manship's reputation. The reviews of the show of his sculptures and drawings held at the Robert Schoelkopf Gallery that same year were similarly scathing, especially the one by John Canaday in the *New York Times*. After that it seemed as though Manship's reputation had sunk too low

187 **ICARUS FALLING**, 1965
Gilded bronze and crystal quartz, 10 x 6 x 5 in. Minnesota Museum of Art, Saint Paul; Bequest of the Estate of Paul Howard Manship

for resurrection. Perhaps the only positive note in all of this was that his enemies still thought him worthy of attack.

Throughout art history, the most unlikely reputations have been revived: El Greco, Piero della Francesca, Vermeer, and Georges de La Tour are just a few artists who suffered centuries of oblivion. John Singer Sargent was vilified after his death, and it took more than thirty years for the wheel of fashion to turn back to him. And so, too, Manship's reputation started to improve in the early 1980s, heralded by a rise in his auction prices, and the revival has continued steadily ever since. The Minnesota Museum of Art, which had previously exhibited only one or two of the several hundred pieces they had been bequeathed, organized a traveling exhibition in 1985 to commemorate the centennial of Manship's birth, and the National Museum of American Art mounted another major show in 1989.

In the introduction to the catalog for the exhibition at the Schoelkopf Gallery in 1971, John had compared his father's position in American twentieth-century sculpture with that of Jean-Auguste-Dominique Ingres in French art of the nineteenth. Both had begun their careers as mild revolutionaries; both had studied in Rome and never escaped from its influence; and in their old age both had set themselves against radical tendencies, a stance that led them to be criticized and abused. But now Ingres's greatness is recognized, as we will also come to recognize Manship's. In particular, the small bronzes modeled originally in wax are among the purest, most poetic sculptures done since the Renaissance (plates 181–83, 187, 188). In them flowered Manship's gift for imaginative composition and his ability to concentrate invention into a small format.

Perhaps Gutzon Borglum was partly right when he called Manship a mouse. Although Manship did enough big work to disprove Borglum's characterization, in the long run he was happiest with the small. Paul Manship believed it essential for a sculptor to be complete by exercising his talents in all genres. He tried almost everything, and even when his work was unsuccessful it was distinctively his own, for his style united all his disparate inventions. That style, which began in eclecticism and passed through the stylization of Art Deco, was distilled at the end into a personal expression of the classical tradition.

188 **EURYDICE**, *1935*
Bronze and crystal
quartz, height: 18½ in.

NOTES

I have indicated only references that are in the public record; much of the primary source material for this book is in my files.

1 The genealogist Walter Arps, who has studied the Manship family in eastern Maryland, can find no link between Richard Manship in the seventeenth century and Noah Manship at the end of the eighteenth. There also seems to be some evidence that Richard died childless. However, I think it very unlikely that unrelated people with this unusual name would have settled in eastern Maryland, and no other Manships are recorded as having emigrated from England. Noah didn't spring from nothing, but his descent from Richard cannot be proved.

2 In the family Bible are scrupulously recorded not only the birth dates of the seven children but also the dates of the christenings of the first five. It seems that Mary and Paul were not baptized. This is curious as the Manships had been staunch Methodists since Bishop Asbury had converted the people of eastern Maryland in the eighteenth century. Paul's

nephew William Manship thinks that sometime around 1880 Paul's parents had shifted from the Methodist to the Baptist Church. They thus would have delayed their youngest children's baptisms —in accordance with Baptist precepts—until they could freely choose it themselves. Mary was to do so, but Paul never did.

3 Much of my information concerning Solon Borglum is from A. Mervyn Davies's admirable life of his father-in-law: *Solon H. Borglum: "A Man Who Stands Alone"* (Chester, Conn.: Pequot Press, 1974).

4 Ruth Sherwood [Polašek's wife], *Carving His Own Destiny: The Story of Albin Polašek* (Chicago: Ralph Fletcher Seymour, 1954), contains extensive material on Polašek's stay at the Academy in Rome, at the same time Manship was there.

5 Diederich, in *Catalogue of the First American Exhibition of Sculpture by Hunt Diederich with Introduction by Christian Brinton* (New York: Kingore Galleries, 1920). In her 1986 doctoral dissertation on Manship for the University of Delaware, Susan Rather ex-

plains that Paul lost his temper with Charles Grafly on being bypassed for a job, and this may have contributed to his abrupt departure.

6 Manship believed that he had destroyed this piece, as he had much of his juvenilia, but he must have left it at the family home in Saint Paul when he returned in 1909. Paul K. Manship, the sculptor's nephew, inherited it from his own father, William Manship, and gave it to me.

7 Bennard Perlman found Manship's name on Henri's class list; see William Innes Homer, *Robert Henri and His Circle* (Ithaca, N.Y.: Cornell University Press, 1969), p. 150.

8 Manship's letters to Konti are in the Archives of American Art, Smithsonian Institution.

9 Mrs. Daniel Chester French [Mary Adams French], *Memories of a Sculptor's Wife* (Boston: Houghton Mifflin, 1928), pp. 247–48.

10 Manship never talked about this episode and information about it comes only from his letters to Konti in the Archives of American Art. He did, however, frequently mention his uneasi-

ness at the beginning of his Rome stay. The monument to Governor Johnson was eventually done by Andrew O'Connor.

11 Barry Faulkner, *Sketches from an Artist's Life* (Dublin, N.H.: W. L. Bauhan, 1973), p. 75.

12 Ibid., p. 63.

13 A romanticized version of this episode is to be found in Mrs. Deane McKay's "The Romance of the Duck Girl" in *Woman's Magazine,* November 1914.

14 Isabel later said that no one who hadn't been through the experience of caring for the bedridden could know how excruciatingly difficult and exhausting it was. Her love for Paul was strengthened by his sympathy and kindness to her old father and by the practical aid he rendered in lifting and changing him.

15 The only disappointment of this banner year was Manship's rejection by the National Academy of Design for associate membership. Kenyon Cox, who had proposed him, assured Manship that he would propose his name again and, indeed, in the spring of 1914 he was elected an Associate.

16 Postmaster Morgan was quoted in the *New York Tribune,* January 21, 1914.

17 The newspaper report is, I believe, inaccurate. I find no evidence that Rockefeller purchased the *Centaur and Dryad.*

18 Martin Birnbaum, *Introductions* (New York: Frederic Fairchild Sherman, 1919), pp. 51–58. See also Birnbaum's memoirs, *The Last Romantic* (New York: Twayne, 1960).

19 Royal Cortissoz, *New York Tribune,* February 20, 1916.

20 Paul Manship, unpublished memoir in the author's files.

21 *Spur,* April 15, 1918; *American Magazine of Art,* June 1918.

22 *Freeman,* April 21, 1920; Peyton Boswell, *New York American,* April 11, 1920; Royal Cortissoz, *New York Tribune,* April 11, 1920. Other reviews included Frank Owen Payne, "Two Amazing Portraits by Paul Manship," *International Studio,* October 1920; *Town and Country,* May 1920; and *Arts and Decoration,* May 25, 1920.

23 Manship asked Daniel Chester French if he could borrow his copies of the life mask and hands of Lincoln. When French refused, Adolph Weinman gave him the copies he had, which had come from Augustus Saint-Gaudens. These castings thus served three important sculptors for their statues of Lincoln.

24 The speakers at the dedication ceremony included Senator James Watson of Indiana; Arthur Hyde, the Secretary of Agriculture; Dan Beard, of the Boy Scouts; Ida Tarbell, the Lincoln historian; and others.

25 For a popular history of Rockefeller Center, see Walter Karp, *The Center* (New York: American Heritage Publishing Co., 1982).

26 While Manship was in London, Duveen tried to arrange for him to do a portrait of the Duke of Kent, the younger son of King George V. A schedule of sittings was determined, but Manship eventually decided against doing the work on the grounds that he wouldn't have enough sittings and that he was too busy. The probable reason—as with the aborted portrait of the Prince of Wales a dozen years earlier—was Paul's stubborn American disrespect for England's aristocracy. Because of its rigid caste system, he never liked England very much, certainly not as much as he liked France and Italy, although he had success there.

27 Paul Manship, "Why Established Artists Should Oppose War and Fascism," in *First American Artists Congress* (New York, 1936), pp. 19–20.

28 *Encyclopedia Britannica,* 1941, vol. 20, pp. 198–205 (a history of sculpture) and pp. 215–17 (decorative sculpture).

29 Faulkner, *Sketches,* p. 156.

30 See Carlyle Burrows, "Art of the Week," *New York Herald Tribune,* May 20, 1945, and an article by Rosamund Frost in *Artnews* of June 1945. On the whole, press coverage was slight for so major a show.

31 This episode certainly suggests that Manship had a high opinion of his own worth, which is only natural —how else could he have persevered in his career for over sixty years? But he was modest in his manner and detested those artists—like Frank Lloyd Wright—who were not. One Manship scholar, the late Professor Frederick Leach, frequently quoted Manship as having said: "I had no great talent but was free and unencumbered; I was the right man at the right time" (see *Paul Manship: An Intimate View,* Saint Paul, 1972, and *Paul Manship— Changing Taste in America,* Saint Paul, 1985). The source of this quote is the artist's nephew, the late Paul K. Manship, who cited it as something his uncle had said to him. I am very skeptical of it. Manship certainly was the right man at the right time and knew it, but it is most unlikely that he ever would have said that he had little talent.

32 Paul Manship to Dr. David Scott, October 22, 1965: "Will you please tell me what disposition you plan to make of my sculpture. . . . I should object to my production in sculpture through the years . . . being thrown in with the hoi polloi—to await until water finds its level, if ever. So it is that Ego wishes recognition, and that is why I have chosen the Smithsonian Institution Collection of Fine Arts as the depository of sixty years of work and such pieces of my art as I hope may survive the turbulence of taste and the hasty judgment of contemporaries. . . . Could a Manship room be arranged at the new exhibition building? That is my obvious question to you."

CHRONOLOGY

	EVENTS	PRINCIPAL WORKS

1885　December 24—Paul Howard Manship born in Saint Paul, Minnesota, the youngest and seventh child of Charles H. and Mary Etta Friend Manship. (The date of Manship's birth is often given as December 25, but according to the Manship family Bible he was born on the 24th.)

1892–1900　Attends school.

1900–1903　Studies at Mechanics Arts High School; studies painting and sculpture in evening classes at the Saint Paul School of Art (later known as the Saint Paul Institute of the Arts and Sciences).

1903　Leaves school to work as a designer and illustrator.

1905　Takes train to New York. Attends the Art Students League. Spring—becomes assistant to Solon Borglum.

1907　Summer—meets Isabel McIlwaine; they are engaged later that summer. September 26—mother dies. Fall—leaves Borglum to begin studies at the Pennsylvania Academy of the Fine Arts, Philadelphia.

1908　Leaves the Pennsylvania Academy and returns to New York; becomes assistant to Isidore Konti. July—visits Spain with William Hunt Diederich.

1909　Briefly studies painting with Robert Henri at the New York School of Art. Summer—wins three-year scholarship to the American Academy in Rome. August—visits Minnesota. September—sails to London on the *Lusitania;* visits London, Holland, and Paris before proceeding to the American Academy in Rome.

1910　Summer—travels with Isabel and others to Venice.

1911　February 2—father dies. Summer—Paul travels with Isabel and others to Verona, Florence, and Siena.

     Duck Girl

1912　Spring—visits Greece. Fall—returns to New York.

     Little Brother, Lyric Muse, Playfulness, Satyr and Sleeping Nymph

	EVENTS	PRINCIPAL WORKS
1913	January 1—marries Isabel McIlwaine at Grace Church; they move to an apartment at 1142 Madison Avenue. February—exhibits ten sculptures made in Rome at a show organized by the American Academy and held at the Architectural League, New York. Receives first important commissions for garden and architectural sculpture. December 22—daughter Pauline Frances born in New York. *Centaur and Dryad* awarded Helen Foster Barnett Prize by the National Academy of Design, New York.	*Centaur and Dryad, Saint Joseph, Soldier of the Revolutionary War*
1914	February—exhibits thirteen sculptures at the Pennsylvania Academy of the Fine Arts and is awarded the George D. Widener Memorial Gold Medal for the *Duck Girl*. Spring—elected an Associate of the National Academy of Design, New York. Summer—visits Milan, Venice, Sicily, and Rome.	*Infant Hercules Fountain, Pauline Frances—Three Weeks Old,* sculpture for the American Telephone and Telegraph Company building
1915	March 15—traveling show organized by the Carnegie Institute's Museum of Art opens in Pittsburgh; tours nine cities. Awarded gold medal, Panama-Pacific Exposition, San Francisco. Moves to Washington Mews. Summer—rents house in Cornish, New Hampshire; returns there next two summers.	*Salomé, Spirit of the Chase, Wrestlers*
1916	April 26—elected an Academician of the National Academy of Design. April—visits Bermuda. May 16—meets John Singer Sargent. Gaston Lachaise and Reuben Nakian become his assistants.	*Briseis, Dancer and Gazelles, Flight of Night, Day and the Hours—Sundial*
1917	Awarded Helen Foster Barnett Prize for *Dancer and Gazelles*.	*Indian* and *Pronghorn Antelope* in heroic size
1918	Fall—accepted as a volunteer in the Red Cross and given the rank of lieutenant; sails for London, then takes train to Venice. Catches pneumonia and spends the winter recuperating in Rome.	*John Barrymore, Cycle of Life—Armillary Sphere, David, Hercules Upholding the World—Armillary Sphere, John D. Rockefeller*
1919	February—returns to New York.	
1920	Elected to the National Institute of Arts and Letters, New York.	*John Pierpont Morgan Memorial*
1921	Awarded American Independent Artists Medal and a gold medal from the American Institute of Architects, Washington, D.C. May—sails to London. Fall—moves to Paris. October—meets Bernard and Mary Berenson in Venice and drives with them to their Tuscan villa, I Tatti. November 15—daughter Elizabeth Robinson born in Paris.	*Atalanta, Spear Thrower, Diana*
1921–26	Remains in Paris, with visits to America and Italy.	*Myron T. Herrick, Frederick P. Keppel*
1922–23	Winter—serves as professor of sculpture at the American Academy in Rome.	
1923	First exhibition of his work held in Paris. Gives up lease on house and studio at Washington Mews.	*The Marchioness of Cholmondeley, War Memorial* for the American Academy in Rome

EVENTS	PRINCIPAL WORKS
1924 Rents studio at 6, rue du Val de Grace. February—travels to Crete, Egypt, and Istanbul. Awarded J. Sanford Saltus Medal by the American Numismatic Society.	*Actaeon* and *Diana* in heroic size, *Europa and the Bull*
1925 January—returns to New York for eight months. Buys five brownstones on East Seventy-second and Seventy-third streets. Awarded the gold medal at Philadelphia Art Week. Exhibits at the *Exposition Internationale des Arts Décoratifs et Industriels Modernes,* Paris. May—travels to Saint Paul. August—travels to Brussels and Paris; December—returns to New York.	*Adam* and *Eve, Flight of Europa*
1926 January—begins working in studio in renovated brownstone at 319 East Seventy-second Street, New York. Spring—travels to Paris and Spain (Burgos, Toledo, Avila, Madrid). December—returns to New York and family moves into living quarters at 319 East Seventy-second Street.	*Indian Hunter and His Dog, Soldiers Monument* at Thiaucourt, France
1927 January 16—son John Paul born. Spends summer in Cornish, New Hampshire.	*Designs for the Coinage of the Irish Free State, Venus Anadyomene Fountain*
1928	*Theseus and Ariadne*
1929 Receives Légion d'Honneur. Awarded National Arts Club Prize. June 19 —daughter Sarah Janet born in Paris. Receives commission for equestrian statue of Ulysses S. Grant.	
1931 Becomes a Fellow of the American Academy of Arts and Sciences. Luther Manship dies.	
1932 Elected to the American Academy of Arts and Letters.	*Abraham Lincoln—the Hoosier Youth,* animal details from *Paul J. Rainey Memorial Gateway*
1933 Summer—travels to Paris, the French Alps, and Les Sablettes, France. Returns to New York to prepare for an exhibition of his recent work at Averell House. Winter—works at the American Academy in Rome.	
1934 Spring—returns to New York for dedication of *Prometheus* and the Rainey gates.	*Celestial Sphere, Paul J. Rainey Memorial Gateway, Prometheus Fountain*
1935 Retrospective held at the Tate Gallery, London.	*Eurydice, Orpheus*
1936 May—signs contract to create the *Woodrow Wilson Memorial—Celestial Sphere* for the League of Nations, Geneva. Helps organize the American Artists Congress, New York.	
1937 Receives Diplôme d'Honneur, Paris Exposition. Becomes a member of the Commission of Fine Arts, New York (to 1941). Summer—visits Paris and closes up his studio there.	

EVENTS	PRINCIPAL WORKS

1938   Summer—travels to Paris; rents studio in Montrouge on edge of the city. September—returns to New York.

Moods of Time and *Time and the Fates Sundial* for the New York World's Fair

1939   Elected president of the National Sculpture Society, New York (serves until 1942).

Façade for the Norton Gallery and School of Art, West Palm Beach, Florida; *Woodrow Wilson Memorial—Celestial Sphere*, Geneva

1940   Summer—spends a few weeks on Cape Ann, Massachusetts, as he was to do each subsequent summer (except 1950). Works on sketch for equestrian monument to General James Longstreet (never realized).

1941

Garden of Eden—Sundial

1942   Awarded Medal of Honor, National Sculpture Society. Elected vice president of National Academy of Design (serves until 1948).

1943   Begins teaching at the Pennsylvania Academy of the Fine Arts (until 1947). Buys fourteen acres in Lanesville, Massachusetts, and has house built there.

1944   Becomes Corresponding Member, Academia Nacional de las Bellas Artes, Argentina.

1945   Spring—awarded gold medal for sculpture, National Institute of Arts and Letters.

Hercules

1945–46   Serves as acting president of the National Sculpture Society.

1946   Becomes Corresponding Member, Académie des Beaux-Arts, Paris. Summer—moves into Lanesville house; has a studio built next to the house.

Albert A. Murphree Memorial, Alfred E. Smith Memorial Flagpole Base

1947

Alexander Graham Bell

1948   Elected president of the American Academy of Arts and Letters (serves until 1954). Visits Italy.

John Hancock, Susanna

1949   Summer—travels to Europe.

Spring

1950   Elected president of the Century Club (serves until 1954). Spends summer in Rome. From this year to the end of his life he makes an annual trip to Europe—Florence, Rome, and often Paris—and spends some weeks each summer in Gloucester, Massachusetts.

Isabel Manship, Prometheus Trilogy

1952   Becomes member of the Accademia di San Luca, Rome.

Gateway to the William Church Osborn Memorial Playground, Immortality and *Memory* reliefs for the American Military Cemetery at Nettuno, Italy

EVENTS	PRINCIPAL WORKS
1953	*Alexander Graham Bell* relief, *Comrades in Arms* for the American Military Cemetery at Nettuno, Italy, *Maenad*
1954 Sells properties at Seventy-second and Seventy-third streets; moves to new studio at 10 East Seventeenth Street and apartment at 21 Gramercy Park, New York.	
1955 Breaks a leg; takes a cure at Abano, Terme, Italy.	Four reliefs for the New York Coliseum, *Triptych* for the American Military Cemetery at Nettuno, Italy
1956 Moves to apartment in the National Arts Club, 15 Gramercy Park.	
1957 *Paul Manship,* by Edwin Murtha, is published.	Seals for the Saint Lawrence Power Authority
1958 Moves studio to 901 Broadway.	
1960 Awarded National Arts Club Medal of Honor.	*Memorial to Sam Rayburn, John F. Kennedy Inaugural Medal, Herbert Lehman Gateway* for the Children's Zoo in Central Park, New York, *Leda*
1961 Awarded Medal of Honor by Circolo Artistico, Carrara, Italy, and Premio San Luca by Circolo dei XII Apostoli, Florence. Mary Manship Brown (sister) dies.	
1963 Celebrates golden wedding anniversary.	
1964 Completes Theodore Roosevelt statue in Paris.	*Armillary Sphere* for the New York World's Fair, *Theodore Roosevelt Memorial* (dedicated in 1967)
1965 Redrafts his will. Spends Christmas in Rome.	Studies for *Settlers of the East and West*
1966 January 28—dies in New York. February 8—funeral held at Grace Church.	

SOLO EXHIBITIONS

1913 Architectural League, New York (with Edgar
Williams and Frank Fairbanks), February.
Studio, 27 Lexington Avenue, New York, November
6–8.

1914 Pennsylvania Academy of the Fine Arts,
Philadelphia, February 8–March 2.
Milwaukee Art Society and Minnesota State Art
Society, Saint Paul, March.
Women's Cosmopolitan Club, New York, April 1–
May 22.

1915 Saint Botolph Club, Boston, February 23–March 6.
Carnegie Institute, Museum of Art, Pittsburgh,
March 15–29.
City Art Museum, Saint Louis, April 14–28.
Panama-Pacific Exposition, San Francisco, Summer.
Art Institute of Chicago, August 18–26.
Albright Art Gallery, Buffalo, October 9–November 14.
Detroit Institute of Arts, November 20–December 26.

1916 Cincinnati Art Museum, January.
Berlin Photographic Company, New York, February
15–March 9.
John Herron Art Institute, Indianapolis, March 1–12.
Peabody Institute, Baltimore, April 3–April 9.
Milwaukee Art Society, April 15–May 1.
Bar Harbor, Maine, Summer.
Newport, Rhode Island, Summer.

1920 Corcoran Gallery of Art, Washington, D.C., January.
Scott and Fowles, New York, April 5–17.

1921 Leicester Galleries, London, June 22–July 31.

1923 Exposition d'Art Américain, Paris (with John
Sargent, Winslow Homer, and Dodge MacKnight),
May 18–June 25.

1928 Art Gallery of Ontario, Toronto, April 13–May 6.

1929 California Palace of the Legion of Honor, San
Francisco, July.

1933 Averell House, New York, April 16–May 15.

1935 Tate Gallery, London, June 18–July 31.

1936 Virginia Museum of Fine Arts, Richmond, November
14–December 14.

1937 Corcoran Gallery of Art, Washington, D.C., January
1–31.

1939 Century Association, New York, March 26–April 30.

1942 John Herron Art Institute, Indianapolis, October–
November 8.

1945 Galleries of the American Academy of Arts and
Letters, New York, May 18–December.

1951 Studio, 319 East Seventy-second Street, New York,
April 12–20.

1957 Century Association, New York, January 9–April 8.

1958 Walker Art Center, Minneapolis, November 16–
December 28.
National Collection of Fine Arts, Smithsonian
Institution, Washington, D.C., February 23–March 26.

1966 National Arts Club, New York, May 10–24.
Chesterwood, Stockbridge, Massachusetts, Summer.
National Collection of Fine Arts, Smithsonian
Institution, Washington, D.C., August 10–September 16.

1967 Saint Paul Art Center, January 18–November.

1971 National Collection of Fine Arts, Smithsonian
Institution, Washington, D.C.
Robert Schoelkopf Gallery, New York, March.

1972 Minnesota Museum of Art, Saint Paul, December 7–
March 31, 1973.
Bush Library, Hamline University, Saint Paul,
December 7–March 31, 1973.

1983 National Museum of American Art, Smithsonian
Institution, Washington, D.C., August 15–July 1984.

1985 Minnesota Museum of Art, Saint Paul, May 19–
August 18.
Hudson River Museum, Yonkers, New York,
November 13–January 5, 1986.

1986 Norton Gallery and School of Art, West Palm Beach,
Florida, February 1–March 15.
Currier Gallery of Art, Manchester, New Hampshire,
April 6–June 1.
Dayton Art Institute, Dayton, Ohio, November 9–
January 4, 1987.

1987 Lakeview Museum of Art and Sciences, Peoria,
Illinois, February 8–March 23.
Memorial Art Gallery, Rochester, New York, August
15–October 18.
Telfair Academy of Arts and Sciences, Savannah,
Georgia, November 17–January 3, 1988.

1989 National Museum of American Art, Smithsonian
Institution, Washington, D.C., February 7–July 4,
and tour.
Terra Museum of American Art, Chicago, February
4–April 2.

PUBLIC SITES

Baton Rouge, Louisiana, State Times Building:
  Charles Manship
Boston, Massachusetts, John Hancock Mutual Life
  Insurance Company Building: *John Hancock*
Bryn Mawr, Pennsylvania, Bryn Mawr College:
  M. Carey Thomas, Anna Howard Shaw Memorial
Colorado Springs, Colorado, Spencer Penrose Zoological
  Gardens: *Group of Deer*
Danville, Illinois, *Soldier of the Revolutionary War*
Detroit, Michigan, Detroit Athletic Club: *Victory Overseas*
Fort Wayne, Indiana, Lincoln National Life Insurance
  Company Building: *Abraham Lincoln—the Hoosier Youth*
Garrison Forest, Maryland, Saint Thomas Church:
  Parish Memorial
Great Smoky Mountains National Park, North Carolina,
  Laura Spelman Rockefeller Memorial Tablet
Gainesville, Florida, University of Florida:
  Albert A. Murphree Memorial
Geneva, Switzerland, United Nations Building:
  Woodrow Wilson Memorial—Celestial Sphere
Greencastle, Indiana, DePauw University:
  Senator Albert Beveridge
Ipswich, Massachusetts, Castle Hill: *Griffins*
Massena, New York, New York State Power Authority:
  Seals
Milwaukee, Wisconsin, *Schuchardt Memorial*
Minneapolis, Minnesota, Lincoln Center: *Four Vases*
Murray Hill, New Jersey, Bell Telephone Laboratories:
  Alexander Graham Bell
Nettuno, Italy, American Military Cemetery: *Comrades in
  Arms* and related works
New Haven, Connecticut, Yale University:
  Phelps Memorial Tablet
New York, New York, Alfred E. Smith Park:
  Alfred E. Smith Memorial Flagpole Base
New York, New York, Bronx Zoo: *Paul J. Rainey Memorial
  Gateway*

New York, New York, Central Park: *Herbert Lehman
  Gateway for the Children's Zoo*
New York, New York, Equitable Center: *Day*
New York, New York, Federal Hall: *George McAneny
  Memorial*
New York, New York, Grant's Tomb: *Ulysses S. Grant*
New York, New York, Little Church around the Corner:
  Otis Skinner Memorial
New York, New York, Coliseum: *Seals*
New York, New York, 195 Fifth Avenue: Decorative
  sculptures
New York, New York, Rockefeller Center: *Prometheus
  Fountain* and related works
Paris, France, Père Lachaise Cemetery: *De Bocande
  Memorial*
Philadelphia, Pennsylvania, Logan Square: *Celestial Sphere*
Philadelphia, Pennsylvania, Rittenhouse Square: *Duck Girl*
Pittsburgh, Pennsylvania, City Hall: *Woodrow Wilson
  Memorial Tablet*
Providence, Rhode Island, Church of the Blessed Sacrament:
  Saint Joseph
Rome, Italy, American Academy in Rome: *Infant Hercules
  Fountain; War Memorial*
Saint Paul, Minnesota, Como Park: *Indian Hunter and
  His Dog*
Saint Paul, Minnesota, Minnesota Mining and
  Manufacturing Company: *Tablet of Founders*
Thiaucourt, France, American Military Cemetery:
  Soldiers Monument; Funerary Urn
Washington, D.C., Rayburn Office Building: *Sam Rayburn*
Washington, D.C., Roosevelt Island: *Theodore Roosevelt*
Washington, D.C., U.S. Postal Service Building:
  Samuel Osgood
West Palm Beach, Florida, Norton Gallery and School of
  Art: *Imagination, Inspiration, Interpretation*

PUBLIC COLLECTIONS

Amherst, Massachusetts, Mead Art Museum
Andover, Massachusetts, Addison Gallery of American Art,
   Phillips Academy
Annapolis, Maryland, United States Naval Academy Museum
Ann Arbor, Michigan, University of Michigan Museum of Art
Bloomfield Hills, Michigan, Cranbrook Academy
   of Art Museum
Bloomington, Indiana, Indiana University Art Museum
Boston, Massachusetts, Isabella Stewart Gardner Museum
Boston, Massachusetts, Museum of Fine Arts
Buffalo, New York, Albright-Knox Art Gallery
Cambridge, Massachusetts, Fogg Art Museum
Chicago, Illinois, Art Institute of Chicago
Cincinnati, Ohio, Cincinnati Art Museum
Cleveland, Ohio, Cleveland Museum of Art
Colorado Springs, Colorado, Colorado Springs
   Fine Arts Center
Columbus, Ohio, Columbus Museum of Art
Dayton, Ohio, Dayton Art Institute
Denver, Colorado, Denver Art Museum
Detroit, Michigan, Detroit Institute of Arts
Fort Wayne, Indiana, Fort Wayne Museum of Art
Fort Worth, Texas, Amon Carter Museum
Gloucester, Massachusetts, Cape Ann Historical Association
Hartford, Connecticut, Wadsworth Atheneum
Honolulu, Hawaii, Honolulu Academy of Arts
Houston, Texas, Museum of Fine Arts
Indianapolis, Indiana, Indianapolis Museum of Art
Jackson, Mississippi, Mississippi Museum of Art
Kansas City, Missouri, Nelson-Atkins Museum of Art
Los Angeles, California, Los Angeles County Museum of Art
Louisville, Kentucky, J. B. Speed Art Museum
Miami Beach, Florida, Bass Museum of Art
Minneapolis, Minnesota, Minneapolis Institute of Arts
Minneapolis, Minnesota, Walker Art Center
Muncie, Indiana, Ball State University Art Gallery
Murrells Inlet, South Carolina, Brookgreen Gardens
New Britain, Connecticut, New Britain Museum of
   American Art
New Haven, Connecticut, Yale University Art Gallery
New York, New York, American Museum of Natural History
New York, New York, American Numismatic Society
New York, New York, Art Students League
New York, New York, Century Association

New York, New York, Columbia University Club
New York, New York, Metropolitan Museum of Art
New York, New York, Museum of the City of New York
New York, New York, National Academy of Design
New York, New York, National Arts Club
New York, New York, New-York Historical Society
New York, New York, Theodore Roosevelt House
Northampton, Massachusetts, Tryon Gallery of Art
Omaha, Nebraska, Joslyn Art Museum
Paris, France, National Collections
Philadelphia, Pennsylvania, Pennsylvania Academy
   of the Fine Arts
Philadelphia, Pennsylvania, Philadelphia Museum of Art
Pittsburgh, Pennsylvania, Carnegie Museum of Art
Portland, Maine, Portland Museum of Art
Poughkeepsie, New York, Vassar College Art Gallery
Providence, Rhode Island, Museum of Art, Rhode Island
   School of Design
Richmond, Virginia, Virginia Museum of Fine Arts
Rockland, Maine, William A. Farnsworth Library
   and Art Museum
Saint Louis, Missouri, Saint Louis Art Museum
Saint Paul, Minnesota, Minnesota Museum of Art
San Antonio, Texas, Marion Koogler McNay Art Museum
San Francisco, California, California Palace of the
   Legion of Honor
Santa Barbara, California, University Art Museum
Seattle, Washington, Seattle Art Museum
South Bend, Indiana, Snite Museum of Art
Terre Haute, Indiana, Sheldon Swope Art Gallery
Toledo, Ohio, Toledo Museum of Art
Toronto, Canada, Art Gallery of Ontario
Tulsa, Oklahoma, Thomas Gilcrease Institute of American
   History and Art
Washington, D.C., Corcoran Gallery of Art
Washington, D.C., Hirshhorn Museum and Sculpture
   Garden, Smithsonian Institution
Washington, D.C., National Gallery of Art
Washington, D.C., National Museum of American Art,
   Smithsonian Institution
Washington, D.C., National Portrait Gallery, Smithsonian
   Institution
Yonkers, New York, Hudson River Museum

SELECTED BIBLIOGRAPHY

UNPUBLISHED SOURCES

Paul Manship Papers. Archives of American Art, Smithsonian Institution. N 714–16: Personal calendars, 1925–35 and 1937–61; N 717: Personal calendars, 1963–65; N 62: Scrapbooks; NY 59–15: Photographs, exhibition catalogs, clippings, writings, lectures, articles on sculpture, etc.; NY 59–16: Writings on art, family records, correspondence, 1933–57, and correspondence A–N, 1940–47; NY 59–17: Correspondence O–Z, 1940–47.

Rather, Susan. "The Origins of Archaism and the Early Sculpture of Paul Manship." Ph.D. diss., University of Delaware, 1986.

MONOGRAPHS AND SOLO-EXHIBITION CATALOGS

Averell House. *Sculpture by Paul Manship.* New York, 1933.

Berlin Photographic Company. *Catalogue of Sculpture by Paul Manship.* Introduction by Martin Birnbaum. New York, 1916.

Brookgreen Gardens. *Sculpture by Paul Manship.* New York, 1938.

Gallatin, Albert Eugene. *Paul Manship: A Critical Essay on His Sculpture, and an Iconography.* New York: John Lane, 1917.

Mead, Franklin B. *Heroic Statues in Bronze of Abraham Lincoln: Introducing the "Hoosier Youth" of Paul Manship.* Fort Wayne, Ind.: Lincoln National Life Insurance Company, 1932.

Minnesota Museum of Art. *Paul Howard Manship, An Intimate View: Sculpture and Drawings from the Permanent Collection of the Minnesota Museum of Art.* Text by Frederick D. Leach. Saint Paul, 1972.

———. *Paul Manship—Changing Taste in America.* Essays by Harry Rand, Frederick D. Leach, Susan Rather, Gurdon L. Tarbox and Robin R. Salmon, William M. Stott, and John Manship. Saint Paul, 1985.

———. *Drawings by Paul Manship.* Text by Carol Hynning Smith. Saint Paul, 1987.

Murtha, Edwin. *Paul Manship.* New York: Macmillan, 1957.

National Arts Club. *Paul Manship Memorial Exhibition.* New York, 1966.

National Collection of Fine Arts, Smithsonian Institution, and Saint Paul Art Center. *Paul Manship, 1885–1966.* Washington, D.C., 1966.

National Museum of American Art, Smithsonian Institution. *Paul Manship.* Text by Harry Rand. Washington, D.C.: Smithsonian Institution Press, 1989.

National Sculpture Society. *Paul Manship.* New York: W. W. Norton and Company, 1947.

Smithsonian Institution. *A Retrospective Exhibition of Sculpture by Paul Manship.* Text by Thomas M. Beggs. Washington, D.C., 1958.

Squire, C. B. *Outdoor Sculpture by Paul Manship.* Wilton, Conn.: Kenneth Lynch and Sons, n.d.

Vitry, Paul. *Paul Manship, Sculpteur américain.* Paris: Editions de la Gazette des Beaux-Arts, 1927.

ARTICLES ABOUT PAUL MANSHIP

Adams, Herbert. "Paul H. Manship." *Art and Progress,* November 1914.

"The Art of Mr. Manship." *Lady's Pictorial,* June 15, 1921.

Arts and Decoration, May 25, 1920.

Beatty, Albert R. "Lincoln the Youth in Bronze." *National Republic,* April 1933.

Boswell, Peyton. *New York American,* April 11, 1920.

Breck, Joseph. "Playfulness." *Bulletin of the Minneapolis Institute of Arts,* October 1914.

Burrows, Carlyle. "Art of the Week." *New York Herald Tribune,* May 20, 1945.

"By the American Sculptor Showing at the Tate." *Illustrated London News,* June 29, 1935.

Caffin, Charles H. *New York Evening Journal,* February 13, 1913.

———. *New York American,* February 9, 1915.

Canfield, Mary Cass. "The Sculpture of Paul Manship: An Evaluation of His Position in Modern Art." *Vanity Fair,* October 1918.

Casson, Stanley. "The Sculpture of Paul Manship." *Listener,* July 10, 1935.

Cortissoz, Royal. *New York Tribune,* May 8, 1914.

———. *New York Tribune,* February 20, 1916.

———. *New York Tribune,* April 11, 1920.

Cox, Kenyon. "A New Sculptor." *Nation,* February 13, 1913.

de Cisneros, Francis G. "La Maciza Escultura de Paul Manship." *Social,* October 1918.

de Cuevas, George. "Paul Manship." *La Renaissance,* July–September 1932.

de Monvel, Bernard Boutet. "La Sculpture décorative de Paul Manship." *Art et industrie,* December 10, 1927.

Ellis, F. L. "Manship's Freedom Stamp Design Was Photo of a Plaster Cast." *Don Housewworth's International Stamp Review,* April 1943.

Ellis, Joseph Bailey. "Paul Manship in the Carnegie Institute." *Carnegie Magazine,* September 1937.

"The Fabulous Fountain." *New Yorker,* October 27, 1934.

"*The Four Elements* by Paul Manship." *Vanity Fair,* November 1914.

"Four Terracotta Portraits by Paul Manship." *Town and Country,* April 15, 1927.

Frost, Rosamund. "Manship Ahoy!" *Artnews,* June 1945.

Gallatin, Albert Eugene. "The Greatness of Paul Manship." *Arts and Decoration,* April 1916.

———. "The Sculpture of Paul Manship." *Bulletin of the Metropolitan Museum of Art,* October 1916.

———. "An American Sculptor: Paul Manship." *Studio,* October 1921.

Goode, James M. "Paul Manship's Greco-Deco Returns." *Museum and Arts, Washington,* January–February 1989, p. 31.

Hancock, Walker. "Paul Manship.'' *Fenway Court* (Bulletin of the Isabella Stewart Gardner Museum), October 1966.

"Heroic Garden Sculptures by Paul Manship." *Vanity Fair,* May 1919.

Hind, C. Lewis. "Paul Manship." *Saturday Review,* July 2, 1921.

Humber, George. "Paul Manship." *New Republic,* March 25, 1916.

Kammerer, Herbert L. "In Memoriam: Paul Manship." *National Sculpture Review,* Winter 1965–66.

———. "Paul Manship, Fourteenth President, National Sculpture Society." *National Sculpture Review,* Fall 1966.

"Lincoln Statue, Fort Wayne." *American Magazine of Art,* September 1932.

McClinton, Katherine Morrison. "Paul Manship: American Sculptor." *Art and Antiques,* March–April 1982.

"Mainstream Bang." *New Yorker,* November 14, 1942.

"The Man Who Makes Bronze Look Alive." *My Magazine,* April 1922.

Manship, Paul. "The Sculptor at the American Academy in Rome." *Art and Archeology,* February 1925.

"The Manship War Medal." *Spur,* April 15, 1918.

Maraini, Antonio. "Lo Scultore Paul Manship." *Dedalo,* August 1923.

"Mr. Manship's Kultur Medal." *American Magazine of Art,* June 1918.

"Mr. Rockefeller, Mr. Manship and Mr. Bernard." *Art and Decoration,* May 25, 1920.

"The Memorial to John Pierpont Morgan." *Vanity Fair,* January 1921.

Metropolitan Magazine, February 1914.

"A Modern Primitive in Art." *Literary Digest,* May 6, 1916.

National Sculpture Review. Manship's works were extensively reproduced and discussed in issues from 1952 to 1987.

"A New Sculptor." *Outlook,* February 14, 1914.

"Patriotic Insignia by Paul Manship." *Harper's Bazaar,* December 1918.

"Paul J. Rainey Memorial Gates." *Architecture,* September 1934.

"Paul Manship—A Conversation." *Craft Horizons,* November 1942.

"Paul Manship at the National Museum." *Antique Almanac,* September 1983.

"Paul Manship at the National Museum." *Apollo,* November 1983.

"Paul Manship in a New Mood." *Vanity Fair,* July 1927.

"Paul Manship, Sculptor." *Photo Review,* July 1945.

"Paul Manship's Dramatic Vision of John D. Rockefeller." *Current Opinion,* July 1920.

"Paul Manship's Exhibition at Scott and Fowles." *Arts,* March 1925.

"Paul Manship's *Lincoln.*" *Vanity Fair,* June 1932.

"Paul Manship's Vision." *Freeman,* April 21, 1920.

"Paul Manship's Work in Sculpture." *Outlook,* March 8, 1916.

Payne, Frank Owen. "Two Amazing Portraits by Paul Manship." *International Studio,* October 1920.

Poatgieter, A. Hermina. "Paul Manship, Sculptor." *Gopher Historian,* Winter 1967–68.

Rainey, Ada. "Sculpture by Paul Manship." *Century Magazine,* April 1913.

———. "A New Note in Art." *Century Magazine,* June 1915.

Rogers, Cameron. "The Compleat Sculptor." *New Yorker,* September 1, 1928.

Rubins, D. K. "Bronze by Paul Manship: *Rape of Europa.*" *Bulletin of the John Herron Art Institute,* April 1951.

Ruiz, E. Gallo. "Medal of Dionysus." *Numismatist,* March 1944.

"Sculpture by Paul Manship." *Century Magazine,* April 1913.

"Sculpture by Paul Manship." *Vanity Fair,* March 1914.

"The Sculpture of Paul Manship." *Harper's Weekly,* March 11, 1916.

"Some Garden Sculpture of Paul Manship." *Country Life,* November 1917.

"A Tablet Erected by the Trustees in Memory of the Late J. Pierpont Morgan." *Bulletin of the Metropolitan Museum of Art,* 1920.

Town and Country, May 1920.

Van Rensselaer, Mariana Griswold. "Pauline." *Scribner's Magazine,* December 1916.

Warren, Louis A. "Lincoln the Youth." *Kiwanis Magazine,* February 1933.

"Who's Who in Minnesota Art Annuals—Paul Manship." *Minnesotan,* July 1915.

Wilson, Malin. "Paul Manship: The Flight of Night." *Museum News* (Toledo Museum of Art), 1974.

"The Works of Paul Manship on View." *Antiques and the Arts Weekly,* August 19, 1983.

GENERAL BOOKS AND ARTICLES

Adams, Adeline. *The Spirit of American Sculpture.* New York: National Sculpture Society, 1923.

Albright-Knox Art Gallery. *Painting and Sculpture from Antiquity to 1942 in the Albright-Knox Art Gallery.* Text by Steven A. Nash. New York: Rizzoli, 1979.

American Art at Amherst (catalog of the Mead Art Gallery collection). Middletown, Conn.: Wesleyan University Press, 1978.

American Battle Monuments issue. *National Sculpture Review,* Winter 1955.

Association Franco-Américaine d'Expositions de Peinture et de Sculpture. *Exposition d'art américain.* Paris, 1923.

Baxter, Barbara. *The Beaux-Arts Medal in America.* New York: American Numismatic Society, 1987.

Birnbaum, Martin. *Introductions.* New York: Frederick Fairchild Sherman, 1919.

———. *The Last Romantic.* New York: Twayne, 1960.

Broder, Patricia Janis. *Bronzes of the American West.* New York: Harry Abrams, 1974.

Bulletin of the Detroit Museum of Art, November–December 1916.

Bulletin of the Museum of Fine Arts, Houston, Texas, June 1940.

Cahill, Holger. *American Art Today.* New York: Harcourt, Brace and Company, 1932.

Calder, A. Stirling. *The Sculpture and Mural Decorations of the Exposition.* San Francisco: Paul Elder Co., 1915.

Casson, Stanley. *Twentieth-Century Sculptors.* London: Oxford University Press, 1930.

A Century of American Sculpture: Treasures from Brookgreen Gardens. Introduction by A. Hyatt Mayor. New York: Abbeville Press, 1981.

Cheney, Sheldon. *A Primer of Modern Art.* New York: Boni and Liveright, 1924.

Coen, Rena Neumann. *Painting and Sculpture in Minnesota, 1820–1914.* Minneapolis: University of Minnesota Press, 1976.

Cortissoz, Royal. *American Artists.* New York: Charles Scribner's Sons, 1923.

Craven, Wayne. *Sculpture in America.* Newark, Del.: University of Delaware Press, 1984.

Davies, A. Mervyn. *Solon H. Borglum: "A Man Who Stands Alone."* Chester, Conn.: Pequot Press, 1974.

Dodd, Loring Holmes. *Golden Moments in American Sculpture.* Cambridge, Mass.: Dresser, Chapman and Grimes, 1967.

Durman, Donald Charles. *He Belongs to the Ages: The Statues of Abraham Lincoln.* Ann Arbor, Mich.: Edwards Brothers, 1951.

Eisler, Colin. *Sculptors' Drawings over Six Centuries, 1400–*

1950. New York: Agrinde Publications, 1981.

Ellis, F. L. "Designs Submitted for the U.N. and Four Freedoms Postage Stamp." *Stamps,* June 16, 1943.

Evert, Marilyn, and Vernon Gay. *Discovering Pittsburgh's Sculpture.* Pittsburgh: University of Pittsburgh Press, 1983.

"Exhibition of Sculpture at the Albright Art Gallery." *Academy Notes,* January 1916.

"Exhibitions at the Art Institute." *Fine Arts Journal,* October 1915.

Failing, Patricia. *Best-Loved Art from American Museums.* New York: Clarkson N. Potter, 1983.

Fairmont Park Art Association, Philadelphia. *Sculpture of a City: Philadelphia's Treasures in Bronze and Stone.* New York: Walker Publishing, 1974.

Faulkner, Barry. *Sketches from an Artist's Life.* Dublin, N.H.: W. L. Bauhan, 1973.

Fink, Lois Marie, and Joshua C. Taylor. *Academy—The Academic Tradition in American Art.* Washington, D.C.: Smithsonian Institution Press, 1975.

Gallatin, Albert. *The Pursuit of Happiness.* New York: privately printed, 1950.

Gayle, Margot, and Michele Cohen. *Guide to Manhattan's Outdoor Sculpture.* New York: Prentice-Hall, 1988.

Goode, James M. *The Outdoor Sculpture of Washington, D.C.* Washington, D.C.: Smithsonian Institution Press, 1974.

Hancock, Walker. "The American Academy in Rome." *National Sculpture Review,* Winter–Spring 1963–64.

Hirschl and Adler. *Carved and Modeled: American Sculpture, 1910–1940.* New York, 1982.

Isabella Stewart Gardner Museum. *Sculpture in the Isabella Stewart Gardner Museum.* Boston, 1977.

Jackman, Rilla Evelyn. *American Arts.* Chicago: Rand, McNally, 1928.

James, Juliet. *Sculpture of the Exposition Palaces and Courts* (on the Pan-American Exposition). San Francisco: H. S. Crocker, 1928.

Kroll, Leon. *A Spoken Memoir.* Edited by Fredson Bowers and Nancy Hale. Charlottesville: University of Virginia Press, 1983.

"London Art Galleries." *Architect,* July 15, 1921.

Lynch, Kenneth. *Sundials and Spheres.* Architectural Handbook Series. Canterbury, Conn.: Canterbury Publishing, 1971.

Manship, John. "Herbert Lewis Kammerer." *National Sculpture Review,* Spring 1981.

Manship, Paul. "Why Established Artists Should Oppose War and Fascism." In *First American Artists Congress.* New York, 1936.

———. "Sculpture" and "Decorative Sculpture." In *Encyclopedia Britannica,* vol. 20, pp. 198–205 and pp. 215–17, respectively. Chicago and London: Encyclopedia Britannica Co., 1941.

Mayall, R. Newton, and Margaret L. Mayall. *Sundials— How to Know, Use and Make Them.* Boston: Hale, Cushman and Flint, 1938.

Meier, Nellie Simmons. *Lions' Paws.* New York: B. Mussey, 1937.

Meschutt, D. "Portraits of Franklin Delano Roosevelt." *American Art Journal* 18, no. 4 (1986).

Metropolitan Museum of Art. *American Sculpture: A Catalogue of the Collections of the Metropolitan Museum of Art.* Text by Albert T. E. Gardner. New York, 1965.

Michigan State Library. *Biographical Sketches of American Artists.* 5th ed. Lansing, Mich., 1924.

Miller, Alec. *Tradition in Sculpture.* New York and London: Studio Publications, 1949.

Museum of Fine Arts, Boston.

American Figurative Sculpture in the Museum of Fine Arts, Boston. Text by Kathryn Greenthal, Paula Kozol, and Jan Ramirez. Boston: Northeastern University Press, 1986.

National Academy of Design. *A Century and a Half of American Art.* New York, 1975.

National Portrait Gallery, Smithsonian Institution. *President's Medal, 1789–1977.* Introduction by Marvin Sadik. Text by Neil MacNeil. Washington, D.C., 1977.

National Sculpture Society. *Contemporary American Sculpture.* San Francisco: California Palace of the Legion of Honor, 1929.

———. *Exhibition of American Sculpture Catalogue.* New York, 1923.

Nordland, Gerald. *Gaston Lachaise—The Man and His Work.* New York: George Braziller, 1974.

Norton Gallery of Art. *Catalogue of the Collection, Norton Gallery of Art.* West Palm Beach, Fla., 1979.

Parkes, Kineton. *Sculpture of Today,* vol. 1. London: Chapman and Hall, 1921.

Proske, Beatrice. *Brookgreen Gardens, Sculpture.* Brookgreen, S.C.: Brookgreen Gardens, 1943, 2d. ed. 1968.

Rather, Susan. "The Past Made Modern: Archaism in American Sculpture." *Arts Magazine,* November 1984.

Rindge, Agnes. *Sculpture.* New York: Payson and Clarke, 1929.

Robb, David M., and J. J. Garrison. *Art in the Western World.* New York: Harpers, 1942.

Saint Paul Art Center. *Spindrift,* vol. 2, no. 1. Saint Paul, 1967.

"Sculptors by Sculptors." *National Sculpture Review,* Winter 1967–68.

Shapley, John, ed. *The Index of Twentieth-Century Artists.* Vol. 1 (November–December 1933): 30–36; vol. 2 supplement (September 1935): 41; vol. 3 (August–September

1936): 40. New York: College Art Association.

Sherwood, Ruth. *Carving His Own Destiny: The Story of Albin Polašek.* Chicago: Ralph Fletcher Seymour, 1954.

Steffanelli, Elvira. "Artistic Evolution of Medals in the U.S." *National Sculpture Review,* Fall 1971.

Steuben Glass. *Designs in Glass by Twenty-seven Contemporary Artists.* New York, 1940.

Taft, Lorado. *Modern Tendencies in Sculpture.* Chicago: University of Chicago Press, 1921.

Taft, Lorado, and Adeline Adams. *The History of American Sculpture,* new edition. New York: Macmillan, 1930.

Taylor, Joshua C. *The Fine Arts in America.* Chicago: University of Chicago Press, 1979.

University Art Galleries, University of New Hampshire. *A Circle of Friends: Art Colonies of Cornish and Dublin.* Durham, N.H., 1985.

University of Michigan Museum of Art. *Illustrated Catalogue of European and American Painting and Sculpture.* Text by Hilarie Faberman and Karen Wight. Ann Arbor, Mich., 1988.

Vermeule, Cornelius. *Numismatic Art in America.* Cambridge, Mass.: Belknap Press of Harvard University, 1971.

Walker Art Center. *Twentieth-Century Sculpture: Selections from the Permanent Collection.* Minneapolis, 1969.

"We Nominate for Hall of Fame. . . ." *Vanity Fair,* January 1916.

Weinman, Robert A., and Lewis I. Sharp. "A Guide to Gotham's Statues." *National Sculpture Review,* Summer 1976.

Whitney Museum of American Art. *A Sculpture Festival.* New York, 1940.

———. *Two Hundred Years of American Sculpture.* New York, 1976.

"Who's Who in American Art." *Art and Decoration,* January 1918.

INDEX

PHOTOGRAPHY CREDITS
The photographers and sources of photographic material other than those indicated in the captions are as follows: Addison Gallery of American Art, Andover, Massachusetts: plate 82; Charles Anderson, New York: plates 2, 13, 14, 17, 18, 35, 63, 91, 102, 103, 129, 132; Wayne Cozzolino, Philadelphia: plates 23, 135; Michael Lafferty: plates 8, 12, 68, 157, 179; Nikolaus Muray: plate 66; New York Zoological Society: plate 173; Clyde Russ: plate 168; Walter Russell: plates 185, 186; Gordon Tarbox: plates 93, 94, 100, 141, 144; De Witt Ward: plates 114, 125.